D1271642

Kirk Douglas looked like an emperor in 1984

MARDI GRAS and BACCHUS
Something Old, Something New

MYRON TASSIN and GASPAR "Buddy" STALL

Foreword by DOM DELUISE

with photographs by RALPH ROMAGUERA

PELICAN PUBLISHING COMPANY

GRETNA 1984

Copyright © 1984
By Myron Tassin and Gaspar "Buddy" Stall
All rights reserved
ISBN: 0-88289-452-8

Library of Congress Cataloging in Publication Data

Tassin, Myron.
    Mardi Gras and Bacchus.
      1. New Orleans (La.)—Carnival—History. 2. Krewe
of Bacchus (Organization) I. Stall, Gaspar. II. Title.
GT4211.N4T38 1984   394.2′5′0976335   84-3193
ISBN 0-88289-452-8

Special acknowledgment for use of art, maps, or photographs appearing on the following pages: pages 12, 20, 24, 28, 30, 36, and 44, by Henrietta Lumetta; pages 26, 38, and 56, from the Gaspar J. "Buddy" Stall collection; pages 16, 42, 46, 47, 48, and 53, courtesy of the Louisiana State Library; pages 33, 43, and 54, courtesy of the Historic New Orleans Collection; page 37, courtesy of the New Orleans Museum of Art; and page 50, from the Gene Fischer Collection.

For their assistance and support, grateful acknowledgment to: August Perez III, Anthony Brocato, Dr. Mervin Trail, Ella DuMontier, Aurelia Frentz, Ralph Romaguera, Linda Graham, Shirley Tassin, and Brien Lundin, research assistant.

Bacchus photographs by Ralph Romaguera

Manufactured in the United States of America

Published by Pelican Publishing Company, Inc.
1101 Monroe Street, Gretna, Louisiana 70053

To the officers and board members of the Krewe of Bacchus: August Perez III, captain; Peter Moss, vice president and parade marshall; William Connick, secretary; Dr. Allen Copping, treasurer; Owen Brennan, Jr., chairman of the board; and board members James Brennan, Theodore Brennan, Anthony Brocato, James Cooke, Jr., Dr. George Dimitri, John W. Dussouy, Sr., Anthony Fasola, Sal Federico, Hugh E. Humphrey, Jr., Roland Hymel, Jr., Michael O'Keefe, Edwin "Petey" Pigeon, Robert E. Richmond, Ed Taylor, and Dr. Mervin Trail.

Gleason on stage with Southern University coed

Contents

Dom DeLuise

Foreword

The first time I heard about New Orleans and the Mardi Gras, I was a little kid. It all seemed like magical fun, like another world far away and unattainable. Then, as a grownup, I found myself in New Orleans (not at Mardi Gras time) and loved it. Every time I was in the Crescent City, I knew I was in a city that was among my favorites in the world. I love Europe, and New Orleans has that same wonderful Old World feeling: classy and rich in color and kinds of people, with extraordinary foods to sample. I was lucky (I *thought*) to be in New Orleans at times other than during the Carnival season. I made a conscious effort to avoid what I perceived to be a crazy time.

Years went by, and then one day I received a call from Dr. Mervin Trail inviting me to be the King of Bacchus. My very first reaction was to say, "Thank you, but I'm too busy." I must admit I felt a little scared, because I didn't know what might be expected of me. My wife, Carol, said, "Why don't you think about it; it might be fun." And I told Dr. Trail just that: I would get back to him. I had some questions. Could we talk? He was most gracious, and we arranged a meeting in New York which took place with my wife, my sister, my brother, and my 85-year-old mother, Vincenza DeLuise. Dr. Trail and I talked. I was intrigued, and I reluctantly said, "Yes!"

I didn't know it at the time, but I was soon to have the experience of a lifetime. I shall always think of my time in New Orleans as King of Bacchus as one of the finest, most positive, most fun, most human experiences of my life. My wife and my three sons, Peter, Michael, and David, got to come to New Orleans and take part in the celebration. And it's something our family still fondly talks about. My sister and brother also shared the joy, but best of all was my mother being treated like the Queen Mother. Every couple of hours she was crying from the joy of the experience. My mother loves to cry. (We're Italian.)

Now, I have been in show business for a long time, and I have been in front of people a good part of my life. I'm telling you, it was an experience I couldn't even imagine. A million cheering people is an awesome sight. I was stunned and surprised at the city's warm embrace.

The people from the Krewe of Bacchus treated us all like family from the moment we stepped off the plane. The ones I got to meet were all—to the last person—kind, sweet, and caring, and they all made me indeed feel like a *king*. It was the warmest week-long caress from an entire city that this human being has ever felt.

Every gracious evening of our stay had, of course, delicious people, food, and fun. And that's what made it ever so special; fun was ever-present. But the thing that touched my heart the most was the *kindness* that always accompanied it. All of the many people connected with Bacchus seemed to love people.

Being King of Bacchus so impressed me that when I was forming a film company a year or so later, I named it Bacchus Films to remind me always of that wonderful, unforgettable experience I was privileged to have when I risked taking that chance and entered the magical world of Carnival and Mardi Gras.

Thank you, my friends. I'll always be grateful. And thanks, too, for inviting me to write the foreword to this book. Long live Bacchus!

Dom DeLuise

MARDI GRAS and BACCHUS

New Orleanians have a passion for parades.

Part 1

MARDI GRAS
Introduction to Part 1

As a New Orleans historian, public speaker, teacher, and radio-TV host, I am invited to expound on a wide range of subjects relating to our area's colorful history. The subject I am asked to explain most often is the celebration of Mardi Gras in New Orleans and southern Louisiana.

Mardi Gras is competing against heavyweight attractions in a city steeped in history. Consider: New Orleans is the only city in the world with a cuisine all its own. Consider: New Orleans politics is unlike politics anywhere else in the world and has always been the leading sport in New Orleans. Consider: jazz, the first American art form, was born in New Orleans and is still a viable part of the culture. The fact that Mardi Gras comes out on top of such a formidable field is a clear indication of the public interest in this former pagan celebration.

My approach in studying and sharing the history of Mardi Gras has always been to find out "why," for I feel that it's more important to know "why" than to know a specific date. If you understand the "why," you will better appreciate what you see during the celebration and *why* it is happening.

After attending just one Mardi Gras in New Orleans, one will agree that it is truly a remarkable phenomenon. Consider: no one person, governmental agency, or staff of any kind coordinates this single largest annual celebration in the United States of America. Consider: only some 1360 dedicated, over-worked, and (for the most part) unappreciated policemen control a crowd of up to one and a half million people who are allowed to adorn masks and drink alcohol at will. Because of its expertise in crowd control, the New Orleans Police Department is constantly being asked to hold seminars for law enforcement groups from around the world.

MARDI GRAS AND BACCHUS

New Orleans's Mardi Gras is said to be the "largest free show on earth" because there is no admission fee. However, an educated estimate by those responsible for presenting the 1983 parades gauges the total cost to run between $40 and $50 million. But tradition has no price tags.

Mardi Gras has deep-rooted traditions. When City Hall was moved to a new location and the parades were rerouted in front of the new City Hall the crowds did not gather on the new parade route. Instead, they returned to the old City Hall and forced the parades to return to the traditional route.

New Orleans's Mardi Gras is a family time, with little concern for age, color, or creed. In fact, the first Rex, King of Carnival in 1872, was a Jewish man named Lewis J. Salomon.

Mardi Gras is unique in the fact that almost all organizations are called *krewes*, yet the word *krewe* cannot be found in the dictionary. The term is not English or American; it is strictly New Orleans. In what other city can one purchase a "parade ladder" (a stepladder with a seat and a safety bar for children to see over the crowd)? Another uniqueness à la Nouvelle Orleans!

The three primary ingredients in a successful Mardi Gras are floats, maskers with throws, and crowds. Since the first parade, organized by the Krewe of Comus on February 24, 1857, the Crescent City has been blessed with ample quantities of all three. The terms "Carnival" and "Mardi Gras" will be used throughout this text. Please note the difference:

CARNIVAL: A *season* of merriment starting on January 6th and ending the day before Ash Wednesday, which is Mardi Gras. (*Carnival* translated means "farewell to flesh.")

MARDI GRAS: A *day* climaxing the Carnival season whereby people are allowed to fatten up before the Lenten fasting begins. (*Mardi Gras* translated means "Fat Tuesday.")

New Orleans has but two seasons: B.C., "before Carnival," when everyone is getting ready for the big event; and D.C., "during Carnival," when the citizenry is concerned with nothing whatsoever besides celebrating it.

It has been said that the people of New Orleans love Carnival, Mardi Gras and parades to the extreme that if a catastrophe left only two survivors, on the next Mardi Gras one would be costumed and in the street, beating a drum and carrying a banner; the other would be standing aside in costume, drinking a Dixie Beer and hollering, "Throw me something, mister."

GASPAR "BUDDY" STALL

CHAPTER ONE

The Beginning

To understand and, therefore, to fully appreciate the modern Mardi Gras, it is necessary to go back in history an estimated five thousand-plus years to a pagan festival in the Arcadian Hills of Greece.

At that time, winter was not a welcome season. A home was rare; a heated home, non-existent. Medicine was primitive; a simple cold often turned into pneumonia and a quick death. A minor cut left unattended could become infected and gangrenous, leading to a horrible, slow death. Those who did not catch a cold and did not freeze or starve or rot to death had a great deal to be thankful for when spring finally came around. Consequently, survivors held a celebration of thanks to the god of vegetation. They sacrificed a goat and sprinkled its blood upon the fields in thanks to the earth for allowing them to endure the feared and dreaded winter.

At sundown, a priest would chase the naked but joyous sinners across the fields of Arcadia and purge the sins from their bodies by flogging them with a whip made from the skin of the sacrificial animal. Once the cleansing was completed, everyone sat around a fire and partook of a feast. The entree? Sacrificial goat.

Human nature in that age was not much different from what it is today. The more people had, the more they wanted. To petition the god for better crops, they threw flour (a symbol of life) upon the fields along with the goat's blood.

As they wanted more and more, they increased the value of the sacrifice from goats to young virgins. Along with better crops they wanted more fertile women and more fertile animals. Their frenzied celebration grew in size and popularity.

Enter the conquering Roman legions. With little effort, the mighty Roman army conquered the Greeks, took them into slavery and stole their beloved celebration. It would become a favorite pastime for the people of Rome.

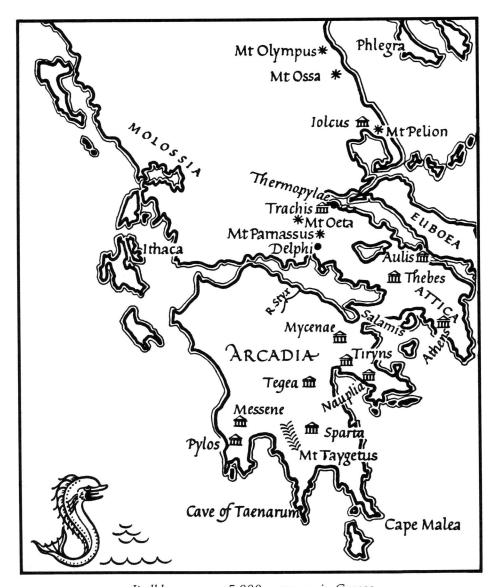

It all began some 5,000 years ago in Greece.

The Roman legions were usually off in distant lands fighting and dying for their emperor. Therefore, the leaders of the empire were constantly organizing activities at home as diversions to placate those with loved ones in the army. As part of this effort to pacify the home populace, Rome constructed the great Coliseum, where chariot races were held with great success. Gladiators were regularly brought in to fight to the death.

The newly pilfered Greek celebration, named Lupercailis by the Romans, served the cause of the empire well; it was an event that the people could participate in, not just watch.

large numbers. This influx of "outsiders," as they were called by the Creoles (white persons descended from early French or Spanish settlers), caused much conflict. As protection for both sides, a neutral ground separating Creoles from Americans was established—a 171-foot-wide area now called Canal Street.

During the 1805 Mardi Gras, tough American river men attended some of the Mardi Gras balls. Fights broke out between the Americans and the Creoles, each side made bolder by the anonymity of costume and mask.

On Ash Wednesday (the day following Mardi Gras) of that year, jails and hospitals were overflowing. The bodies of men who had been stabbed or shot or both were still in the streets. At the same time, the city feared an attack by Aaron Burr, the political radical, who was said to be descending the Mississippi with a sizable force. His supposed intention was to occupy New Orleans and use it as a base to advance his goal of separating the western territory from the United States. Frightened city fathers decided to abolish all Mardi Gras balls and masking.

During the seventeen-year period from 1805 to 1823, there were no legal Mardi Gras balls in the city. And from 1806 to 1827, a period of twenty-one years, Mardi Gras street masking was prohibited.

When the festivities were revived, the old pagan custom of throwing flour was brought back. In 1830, masqueraders riding in carriages tossed little bags of flour, which broke when they struck another masker. This tradition became so popular that on Ash Wednesday, some parts of the city looked as though they were covered with a blanket of snow. Other favorite throws were bonbons and *dragée* (sugar-coated almonds).

Mardi Gras balls also flourished again—to the delight of the Creoles who had a passion for dancing. On Ash Wednesday 1823, the *Orleans Gazette* applauded the revival of the masked balls, explaining in detail the extent to which young ladies would go to attend them. A young American writer reported:

> The day was rainy and disagreeable and the ballroom was situated at the farther extremity of the city. How the ladies were to reach the ballroom we could not divine, as hacks and public vehicles were unknown. But the means proved simple—everything prepared, the order was given to march. The young ladies doffed their shoes and stockings, which were carefully tied up in silk handkerchiefs, and took up a line of march barefooted for the ballroom. After paddling through mud and mire, lighted by lanterns carried by Negro slaves, they reached the scene of action without accident. The young ladies halted before the door and shook one foot after another in a pool of water close by. After repeating this process some half a dozen times, the feet were freed of the accumulated mud and were wiped dry by the slaves, who carried towels for the purpose. Then silk stockings and slippers were put on again, cloaks were thrown aside, tucked up trains were let down, and the ladies entered the ballroom dry shod and lovely in the candlelight.

During the 1839 Mardi Gras, a young Creole gentleman who had returned from school in Europe the previous year tried something novel. He wore a large rooster costume and rode in the back of a horse-drawn vehicle, where he flapped his enormous wings and crowed loudly, to the applause and admiration of the crowd on the sidewalk.

By the 1850s, Americans and Creoles were enjoying Mardi Gras side by side. One writer said Mardi Gras was transformed in the '40s and '50s from an ethnic festival to a celebration of all the people. But this was just the calm before the storm that was to lead ultimately to the birth of the Mardi Gras celebration as we know it today.

CHAPTER THREE

Comus

Just when all seemed to be calm on the New Orleans Mardi Gras scene, the 1856 Mardi Gras proved to be the blackest day in the pageant's history. The weather may have been damp and frigid, but the day's activities were hot and furious. Instead of tossing flour at each other, the maskers threw lime, aiming mostly for the faces of other maskers. In place of bonbons and other sweetmeats, brickbats and similar projectiles were thrown. Newspapers predicted that because of man's continued inhumanity to man, Mardi Gras would once again be outlawed. No one knew it then, but the hostile actions of 1856 would lead not to the demise of Mardi Gras but to the way it has been celebrated from 1857 until today.

What brought about the change? During the hostile times of 1856, six Anglo-Saxon cotton brokers from Mobile, Alabama, were working in New Orleans. Up until this time, Mardi Gras had been, for the most part, a Creole observance that followed French customs and Roman Catholic traditions, feted primarily by masking in the streets, impromptu parades, balls, and general merrymaking.

The cotton brokers were former members of a New Year's Eve parading group called "The Cowbellion de Rakin Society." This group, as the story goes, was organized after a wild party held in Mobile on New Year's Eve 1830. It seems a group of the city's young men were quite inebriated by sunrise of New Year's Day. On their way home, they went past a mercantile store that (as was customary at the time) had some of its wares on the sidewalk out front. The young bacchanals, full of liquid reinforcement and mischief, picked up rakes, shovels, and cowbells and proceeded to raise forty kinds of hell up and down the streets.

They soon found themselves in front of the mayor's home a few blocks away. Being not only a good politician but a master of diplomacy as well, the mayor invited the young men into his home, where he offered them breakfast and strong, black coffee to help the sobering process. He sized up Michael Krafft as the leader of the group and suggested that Krafft organize some form of entertainment the following year for the benefit of all the citizens of Mobile—in exchange for not being thrown into jail.

Krafft took the mayor's suggestion and formed a group that would parade on the following New Year's Eve as the Cowbellion de Rakin Society, a name reflecting the instruments of merriment used in the 1830 outing. On New Year's Eve 1831, the newly-formed group marched in costume, carrying cowbells and rakes.

On March 24, 1857, the Krewe of Comus staged the first organized Mardi Gras parade in the United States.

COMUS

As the years rolled on, the annual pageant added torchlights, but the maskers still marched on foot. In 1840, however, the entire society's parade was on rolling floats and was followed by a ball with a tableau.

The six men who had so much fun in the Cowbellion de Rakin Society decided that unless something was done quickly to preserve Mardi Gras in New Orleans, the festival would be lost forever. They met and prepared a list of the leaders of the city's uptown American section. A short time later, nineteen men met in a room above the Gem Saloon in the 100 block of Royal Street. None of the men were Creoles. This select group nominated a total of eighty-three people to take part in a proposed Mardi Gras pageant. Of the eighty-three, only six had French names.

The next order of business was to choose a name. The Greek name *Komos* was suggested by Dr. John H. Pope, an authority on Greek and Roman mythology. He informed the members that Komos, the god of revelry, would suit their cause admirably. Someone suggested that the Greek name be given an Anglo twist; why not, he said, spell it *Comus* and, at the same time, present a semblance of Greek influence by calling the group a *krewe* instead of a *crew*. Hence, they wound up with "the Krewe of Comus."

Michael Krafft, founder of the Cowbellion de Rakin Society.

Committee chairmen for costumes, floats, flambeaux, music, and ball arrangements were appointed; all committees were filled without delay. A committee was dispatched to Mobile to arrange for the use of two of the Cowbellion de Rakin floats and all of its flambeaux. The request was graciously granted.

For weeks before Mardi Gras, word spread throughout the city that there would be an organized parade with a scheduled time, a specific route, floats with riders, and hundreds of costumed maskers. In addition, colorful flambeaux would light the way for the parade.

After dark on Mardi Gras evening, February 24, 1857, curious people began to fill the streets. The skeptics stayed in the comfort of their homes. And at exactly eight o'clock, on the corner of Julia and Magazine streets, Comus came to life. Within moments, the sky was glowing as if the entire city had been ignited. One person in the crowd was quoted as saying, "It was [as] though they came from within the bowels of the earth, for one minute they were not there, and the next, floats, flambeaux and maskers were just everywhere." Upon seeing the glow from hundreds of flambeaux, those who had decided to stay home were drawn to the parade like ants to a pile of sugar.

The theme of the Comus parade was "The Demon Actors in Milton's *Paradise Lost.*" Paradise might have been lost, but new life for Mardi Gras was found with the birth of the krewe.

The success of the two-float parade was nothing short of phenomenal. Comus, riding high atop his throne on the first float, and Lucifer, on the cone of a blazing volcano on the second, were followed by hundreds of masked marchers. Lighted tapestries, depicting the monstrosities of mankind left the viewers wide-eyed. The sights and sounds of the evening were indelibly etched on the minds of all who witnessed this new, organized spectacle.

After the parade, the group took part in a Mardi Gras ball at the Gaiety Theater. Three thousand guests from New Orleans and Mobile attended. The ball consisted of four spectacular tableaux (depictions of scenes presented on a stage by costumed participants), with accompaniment by Meyer's Orchestra. Dancing was enjoyed by all. To top off the successful evening, a banquet was held for the entire krewe, lasting until early morning. Thus the precedent for all future Carnival parades and balls was established.

The first Comus parade and ball received mostly glowing reports from the local press and a great review from Mark Twain, who witnessed all the festivities. But the Creoles were, to say the least, caustic in their remarks. Upon examining the Comus roster, they found almost every man to be Anglo-Saxon. The parade had been held in the American sector of the city. The Gaiety Theater, site of the ball, was not a Creole favorite, primarily because it was frequented by uptown society.

One of the French language newspapers completely disregarded Comus, as though it hadn't happened. Another suggested that Mardi Gras and Carnival be abandoned at once, implying that the entire event was shifting into the hands of undesirable elements. Yet another French language newspaper denounced Comus as being composed of swine-eating Saxons whose intrusion would bring an end to the city's Mardi Gras festivities.

All of the negative reporting proved to be nothing but sour grapes. The 1857 Comus parade and ball created the format in which Mardi Gras would be celebrated in New Orleans for a long time.

In summary, the first Comus parade and ball made the following contributions:

Coined the word "krewe"
Organized the first secret Mardi Gras society and was first to choose a mythological name
Held the first organized Mardi Gras in the United States with floats, masked riders, flambeaux, and a theme
Held the first Mardi Gras ball with tableaux
Brought law and order back to the New Orleans Mardi Gras, thereby saving it from possible extinction

Krafft's tomb in Mobile with the symbol of the society he founded.

A tombstone of a society member with the cowbell turned down, silenced forever.

CHAPTER FOUR

Twelfth Night Revelers

By the year 1869, the rejuvenation of Carnival and Mardi Gras had transformed the celebration into an orderly, thoroughly enjoyable celebration. So positive was the response that a group of enthusiastic, Carnival-struck New Orleanians decided it was time to add to the enjoyment by forming a second Carnival krewe. The name chosen was "Twelfth Night Revelers," and the group designated the twelfth day after Christmas (January 6) as the official starting day of the Carnival season.

Comus had added new features to the festivities, but the fledgling krewe had a few of its own to inject. On the evening of January 6, 1870, the Twelfth Night Revelers opened the Carnival season with a nine-float parade equal in splendor and pageantry to the previous Comus parades. Hordes of maskers dressed in colorful costumes of Europe, Asia, Africa and America followed on foot.

After the parade, a ball was held at the world-famous French Opera House on Bourbon Street. The king of the Twelfth Night Revelers, dubbed "the Lord of Misrule," reigned over the function. After two tableaux were completed, the Lord of Misrule led his Cleopatra and court in a grand march; they were followed by four court fools carrying an immense king cake. The grand march, the first of the surprises planned by the new krewe (and copied by almost all subsequent krewes), met with tremendous success. Everyone in the packed opera house waited with great anticipation to see what else the Lord of Misrule had up his royal sleeve.

There had never before been a Carnival or Mardi Gras queen. All parades, balls, and tableaux were planned and staged by men. Women did not participate in any fashion until after the tableaux, when they were summoned from the audience to take part in the dancing. But the Twelfth Night Revelers had a great surprise in store: the first queen in the history of the New Orleans Carnival would be chosen, crowned and put upon a pedestal to be admired.

MARDI GRAS AND BACCHUS

The court fools brought out the king cake so that all could witness the selection process. A golden bean had been baked inside the cake; the lady whose piece of cake contained the bean would be chosen queen. The court fools were to slice generous servings of the cake and distribute them to the ladies who waited patiently.

However, all did not go as planned; the court fools lived up to their roles. Having overindulged in liquid libations in preparation for the merriment of the evening, the jesters did not politely dispense the slices. Instead, they dropped them in the laps of the stunned recipients. Some slices were even thrown at the ladies by the more intoxicated jesters. Alas, the bean was not found by anyone.

The following year, 1871, the court fools were better behaved, and a queen, Mrs. Emma Butler, was crowned when she found the golden bean in her slice of cake.

In 1870, the Twelfth Night Revelers introduced the king cake and the grand march to festivities.

TWELFTH NIGHT REVELERS

Despite the king cake mishap, the Twelfth Night Revelers are credited with adding two new aspects to New Orleans' Carnival festivities in 1871: the grand march and the selection of a queen. Both were well received by the participants and adopted by the other krewes that followed.

One can also say that the Twelfth Night Revelers launched the Mardi Gras women's lib movement in 1871, as that was the first time in New Orleans history that the names of female guests at a ball were printed in a newspaper. Up until that time, it was considered undignified for a lady's name to appear in print.

In 1872, Rex rode a horse instead of a float, and the grand duke of Russia declined a throne for a straight-back chair.

CHAPTER FIVE

Rex

His Imperial Highness Alexis Romanoff Alexandrovitch, grand duke of the Russian Empire, lieutenant in the Imperial Navy, and, by birthright, heir to the throne of all the Russias, was scheduled to make a grand tour of the United States and Canada starting in November of 1871. What would he have to do with Mardi Gras? A great deal!

When he arrived in the United States on November 21, 1871, he was officially welcomed in New York City. After meeting with President Ulysses S. Grant and the cabinet of the United States, he attended numerous receptions, balls, plays, parties and banquets held in his honor. With all the necessary protocol in order, he was now ready to begin what he had really come for: a grand tour.

As a tourist, he marveled at Mammoth Cave and was left breathless at the sight of the Grand Canyon. A sports enthusiast whose reputation as a hunter was well known from Indian and African expeditions, the duke wanted to hunt the famed American buffalo that he had read and heard so much about. The hunt, scheduled for Nebraska and Colorado, would include America's greatest buffalo hunter, Buffalo Bill Cody, as a guide for the duke. In deference to Alexis's high station and in order to protect him, United States Generals Philip Sheridan and George Custer were enlisted to go along. To add color to the occasion, a number of Indian chieftains in full regalia were recruited.

His Imperial Highness was very excited and did manage to pull the imperial trigger several times, bringing down several magnificent specimens of the beast. Unfortunately, two enraged bison charged him and almost brought *him* down. His buffalo-hunting desires died quickly.

The grand duke was next taken to see the sights of Niagara Falls where, according to a newspaper account, the sight of the falls made his imperial heart beat faster and even took his breath away momentarily.

From the breathtaking sight of the falls, he traveled to New York City for an event that made his eyes sparkle and brought a broad smile to his normally rigid face. He attended a musical comedy entitled *Bluebeard,* in which the lead was sung by Miss Lydia Thompson, who (it is said) had the voice of an angel. In the play, Lydia sang an absurd little ballad called, "If Ever I Cease to Love."* The grand duke became infatuated with both the silly song and the songstress. He invited Lydia to a late supper that same evening and begged her repeatedly to sing the little ballad that so haunted him. Little did he know that he was setting the stage for the adoption of a royal anthem for Mardi Gras in a city he had never seen and—according to all evidence—had no intentions of visiting.

The next day he inquired about Lydia and was told that she and her troupe were boarding a steamboat heading for performances in Jefferson City, Louisville, Memphis, and New Orleans. The grand duke decided then and there that he had not seen quite enough of the United States, or of Lydia. So when Lydia headed south, so did His Imperial Highness.

Less than two weeks prior to the 1872 Mardi Gras, as Lydia and the grand duke were headed toward New Orleans, a group of approximately forty New Orleans men attended a meeting at the St. Charles Hotel. The meeting had been called by Colonel Walter Merriam, owner and operator of the Crescent City Billiard Hall, and Edward C. Hancock, assistant editor of the New Orleans *Times* newspaper. Upon hearing that the duke was going to honor their city with his presence, these men were excited but concerned. New Orleans was still an occupied city, governed by an unfriendly carpetbag government which had absolutely no comprehension of the term "southern hospitality." The carpet-baggers showed little interest in the important visitor and made no special plans to honor him.

The forty men decided that a new Mardi Gras krewe should be formed to stage a spectacle that would be in keeping with the status of this important guest. The name chosen for the new krewe was Rex; its leader would truly be the King of Carnival.

After much discussion, it was decided that a daylight pageant would be held. The Krewe of Rex would make it a grand procession by inviting thousands of previously unorganized maskers to participate in the spectacle on foot, in wagons, or in carriages. This extravaganza would surely please the grand duke, as well as the people of New Orleans and the thousands of visitors who were sure to come to get a glimpse of the young and debonair prince.

The group outlined a general list of what had to be done. The blessings of the mayor and chief of police were secured. The next order of business was to collect the five thousand dollars needed to stage the event. After the naming of a finance committee, one member, Lewis J. Salomon, took the proverbial bull by the horns. The dedication he showed and the results he got in the short time allowed were extraordinary.

---

*"If ever I cease to love,
 If ever I cease to love,
 May the fish get legs,
 And the cows lay eggs,
 If ever I cease to love."

REX

Next came the moment that everyone was waiting for: who would be selected Rex, the first King of Carnival. The first choice for this coveted position was W. S. Pike, a very successful banker and one of New Orleans's most prominent citizens. He turned down the offer immediately but graciously, feeling that there was not sufficient time to assure a successful presentation. (He did serve as Rex several years later.) The honor was then offered to Lewis J. Salomon, who, convinced that all would go smoothly, accepted without delay. He vowed that he would serve as Rex with the same intensity with which he had served on the finance committee.

The duke's visit to New Orleans prompted the birth of the Krewe of Rex.

There was not enough time to design and tailor a king's costume, so Salomon went to the Variety Theater, where actor Lawrence Barrett allowed him to select a costume from his wardrobe. Appropriately, Salomon picked the costume of Richard III. This costume established the unusual colors of Mardi Gras: the cloak was purple velvet trimmed with rhinestones as green as the sea, and the scepter and crown were gold. (The 1892 Rex parade would be entitled "Symbolism of Colors," with purple representing justice, green signifying faith, and gold indicating power.)

Working in great haste, krewe members next designed a Carnival flag that would be displayed all along the parade route. Purple, green, and gold were employed as follows: a diagonal bar of gold bisected the flag from upper left to lower right, forming an upper triangle of green and a lower triangle of purple. A likeness of the crown of Rex was placed directly in the center.

The new krewe generated interest among and kept its plans before the public with the issuance of daily proclamations in the newspaper. The people were excited about the plans for the grand duke's enjoyment as well as their own.

Each day, edicts came from the palace of the King of Carnival and were published in the newspapers. Some typical pronouncements:

> Rex ordered all private places of business to be closed at 1:00 P.M. on Mardi Gras.
> Rex ordered schools, the post office and the Custom House to be closed and called upon the Louisiana Lottery to close completely on Mardi Gras as well, since the day was consecrated to His Majesty.
> Rex instructed all music groups to play "If Ever I Cease to Love," the royal anthem of Mardi Gras.

Reviewing stands were erected across from City Hall in front of Lafayette Square and decorated in the new Mardi Gras colors. In front of City Hall, a huge canopy of crimson silk outlined with gold fringe and tassels was erected especially for the grand duke. This was no doubt the closest thing to a throne that there was in New Orleans at the time. Wire was strung across the street in front of the reviewing stand, where flags of the United States, Russia, and Rex were to be prominently displayed.

The big day arrived, and so did the grand duke. The weather on February 13, 1872, was absolutely perfect for the outdoor festivities. It was estimated that twenty-five thousand out-of-town visitors had come to New Orleans. Interest had been generated by the newspapers with Rex's proclamations and by carefully placed stories reminding the female population of the chance to see the handsome (and still eligible) twenty-two-year-old grand duke.

MARDI GRAS AND BACCHUS

When Alexis arrived at City Hall, he was offered the seat of honor on the throne, built at great expense for his comfort. He surprised everyone when he adamantly refused to sit upon it and took a seat in a straight-back chair next to Louisiana Governor Henry Clay Warmoth. He was probably concerned about what the czar would think when he saw photographs of his brother sitting on a throne in New Orleans.

The parade started after the firing of a thirteen-gun salute ordered by Rex, His Royal Majesty. Dressed in his purple, green and gold costume, Rex mounted his strutting bay horse. He was followed by a milk-white *boeuf gras* (the fattened ox from pagan times), which was adorned with a gray coverlet on its back and ribbons and flowers on its horns, just as had been done in Rome by the priests of Gallia. Upon reaching City Hall, Rex was presented with the keys to the city by Mayor Benjamin Franklin Flanders.

The parade moved on as five grand divisions, numbering over five thousand, passed in review. First in line were maskers on foot, followed by some in carriages, vans, floats, and other public vehicles. Next came costumed riders on horseback, then stragglers and latecomers, including Dan Rice's troupe of trained animals, Ku Klux Klan impersonators on horseback, shiploads of sailors, and carriageloads of Chinese merchants in authentic costumes.

Some locals who were disenchanted with the city's political situation used the parade to air their feelings by masking in unbecoming costumes representing President Ulysses S. Grant, Abraham Lincoln, and other national figures. Even though Governor Warmoth and Mayor Flanders were on the City Hall reviewing stand with the grand duke, they were not spared abuse. Both were roundly castigated by costumed marchers.

The duke was surely entertained by the grand procession. There is no question that he saw things on that day that he had never seen before or would ever see again. To his great satisfaction, every band in the parade played the Russian national anthem as well as the new royal anthem of Mardi Gras.

The first Rex parade was a smashing success—amazingly, after a planning period of only thirteen days.

But as the old saying goes, you simply cannot please all of the people all of the time. One local newspaper, trying to find fault, wrote that the Rex parade was entirely too well-organized. It sniffed that the people of New Orleans were accustomed to Mardi Gras being more disorganized.

The overwhelming success of the first Rex parade was evident the following year, 1873, when forty thousand visitors came to New Orleans to attend and take part in Mardi Gras—without the attraction of a grand duke. Rex did not disappoint them; an estimated ten thousand masqueraders took part in the parade.

Like the Carnival organizations that had come before them and those that were to follow, Rex made important contributions to Mardi Gras:

> The King of Carnival
> The colors of Mardi Gras
> The flag of Mardi Gras
> The royal anthem of Mardi Gras
> The first use of the *boeuf gras* in a New Orleans Mardi Gras parade
> The first Mardi Gras daylight parade

CHAPTER SIX

Doubloons

The most popular Mardi Gras throw ever—the doubloon—was introduced to Mardi Gras crowds in 1960 and gained immediate approval. This innovation was the brainchild of the late H. Alvin Sharpe. Sharpe was a multi-faceted man: historian, adventurer, ship captain, inventor, and writer. With all his talents, however, it seems that he will only be remembered in New Orleans as the person who mastered the art of intaglio die cutting. (An intaglio is an engraving or incised figure in stone or other hard material in which the design is depressed below the material, so that an impression from the design yields an image in relief.) This ancient art form dates back to the year 700 B.C., when it was mastered by the Greeks and the Persians.

In 1959, Sharpe contacted the Rex organization by mail and advised them that he had designed some very attractive doubloons that could be coined in soft aluminum and produced cheaply in large quantities. He said that, in his opinion, these Rex coins would be sensational mementos of Mardi Gras, and would be harmless to throw to the crowds.

Sharpe's timing was perfect; the Rex captain was at that moment looking for something different to offer to paradegoers. Sharpe was invited to present his design, discuss the matter and demonstrate how the lightweight aluminum doubloons could be thrown from floats without injuring anyone.

Sharpe discussed and demonstrated his idea and walked out of the meeting with an order for 83,000 doubloons: 80,000 aluminum and 3,000 gold anodized. For the first year, the date was purposely left off all but a small percentage. The captain was not sure that krewe members would like the new throw as much as he did, so any leftover doubloons could be used in subsequent years if left undated.

Needless to say, the introduction of doubloons to Mardi Gras crowds met with immediate success. In fact, in just a few years, the cry of Carnival crowds turned completely from "hey mister, throw me something" to "hey mister, throw me a doubloon." Their popularity was so great that between 1960 and 1970, Rex threw 2.75 million of them to chanting, doubloon-crazy crowds. Most of the other krewes joined in on Rex's success and ordered doubloons minted for their own use. As the captain of Rex said, imitation is the greatest form of flattery.

At first, doubloons were only struck in aluminum and anodized gold. As time passed, however, doubloons in all colors of the rainbow were minted for various krewes. From aluminum doubloons, the art progressed to the more precious metals of silver, nickel, copper, bronze and sterling silver; the costlier ones were usually given to very special friends or guests at the balls. Some doubloons were made thicker, and these were likewise used as special favors to be given, not thrown. Soon doubloons changed from solid-colored to multi-colored and were given ceramic coatings to protect them. The most recent innovation has been the minting of doubloons in various shapes: shields, flowers, hearts, Christmas trees, and others.

(The change from the original colors of gold and aluminum was readily accepted. People thought nothing of having an array of colors on a single doubloon and even accepted doubloons coated with ceramics. But for some strange reason, when the various shapes started hitting the streets, the crowds labeled them un-doubloons. Tradition!)

The first Rex doubloon

Since 1960, four to five thousand different Carnival doubloons have been struck and minted, to be thrown or given to anxious crowds. With 2.75 million being thrown by just one krewe in eleven years, it is easy to see that if the craze continues at the present level, there could soon be a billion doubloons floating around the city of New Orleans. Of course, some will be carried to all corners of the world by those who visit during Carnival, perhaps serving as seeds to get others to come to the biggest "free" show on earth.

It is possible that *doubloon* is not really the correct term for the medallions thrown from carnival floats. A doubloon is defined as an old gold coin of Spain or Spanish America. A coin is a piece of metal issued by governmental authority as money. The definition of a medal is a coin-shaped piece of metal not issued as money but struck to preserve the portrait of a person or the memory of some important occasion. But one thing is certain. Not even a massive, multi-million-dollar campaign could change the name of the medallion thrown at Carnival from *doubloon* to anything else.

In 1885, Rex did have a coin-shaped piece of metal struck to preserve an important event: the 1884 World's Fair held in New Orleans. On one side of the coin is a replica of the Rex coat of arms, and on the other side is an image of the main building of the 1884 World's Fair. Therefore, in the present context of the word *doubloon,* it would be correct to say that the first New Orleans Mardi Gras doubloon was actually given out, not thrown, by Rex in 1885.

Most New Orleanians are eternally grateful to Sharpe for adding to the enjoyment of the Mardi Gras season by applying his talents to this innovation. His intent was to offer a throw that was truly beautiful, easy to throw, inexpensive and safe. In three of the four areas he was successful; the safety factor is debatable. Sweet old gray-haired grandmothers seem to go crazy when a doubloon hits the sidewalk and makes its tinkling sound. These normally timid folks have been known to stomp the fingers of anyone who tries to retrieve a doubloon in their vicinity. Even their own grandchildren are advised to be careful.

But life is a gamble! To attend a Carnival parade without catching a doubloon would be as sinful as coming to New Orleans without eating a plate of red beans and rice, listening to jazz music, or visiting the French Quarter.

The main building of the 1884 World's Fair, featured on one side of the Rex doubloon, was four times as large as the Superdome.

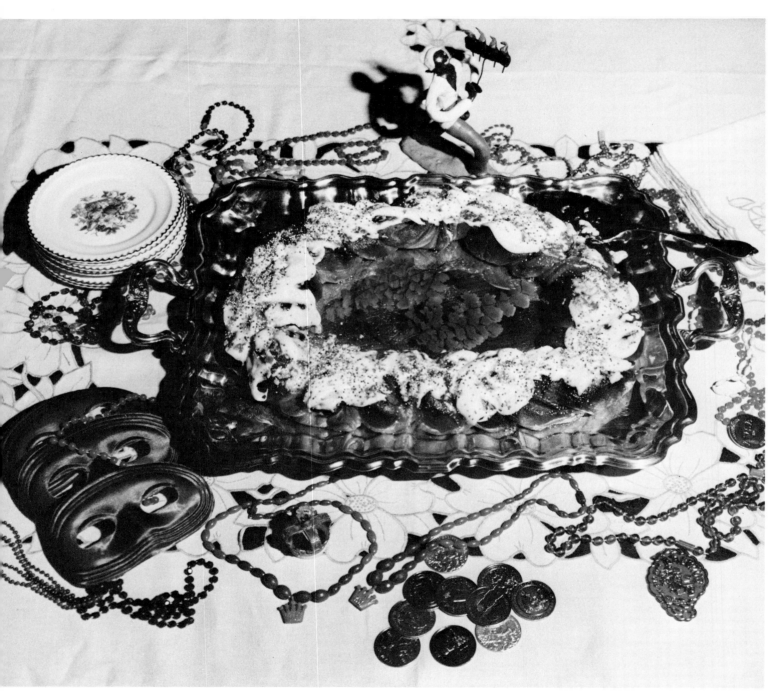

In 1983, between 450,000 and 500,000 king cakes were consumed during the Carnival season in New Orleans.

CHAPTER SEVEN

King Cake

Although the king cake (originally called "kings cake") has been part of the Carnival scene in New Orleans since the Twelfth Night Revelers' first ball, it really did not reach its pinnacle of popularity until about the early 1970s. From only a handful in the early years, sales have soared to hundreds of thousands. Over 250,000 were sold in 1983 by just one of the many prolific local bakeries.

The story of the king cake begins, like the story of Mardi Gras itself, with the pagans. They had a celebration whereby a young man in the village was chosen to be treated like a king for a full year. He was denied absolutely nothing during his reign, but after the year was over, he became a human sacrifice to the gods.

To thwart this pagan custom, the Christian Church encouraged an observance calling for the preparation of a king cake containing a bean; whoever received the slice with the bean became king for a week and was allowed to choose a queen to reign with him. In time, this simple tradition replaced the sacrificial pagan rite.

When the first queen of Mardi Gras was chosen by the Twelfth Night Revelers on January 6, 1870, the means of selection was the king cake. Twelfth Night, also known as King's Day (Epiphany, January 6), is the twelfth night after Christmas—the night when the three kings brought gifts to the Christ Child. The Revelers brought the Christian king cake tradition to New Orleans and were responsible for linking the cake with Carnival for the first time ever on that night in 1870.

Today, the Twelfth Night Revelers still use the king cake tradition in choosing their queen and her court. In place of a real cake, however, an artificial cake with small drawers is used. One drawer holds a gold bean; the rest contain silver beans. The young woman selecting the drawer with the gold bean is crowned queen, and those selecting silver are her maids.

Over the years, the items in real king cakes indicating who will be king have changed. A bean was originally used, but was replaced in subsequent years by coins, peas, pecans, rubber dolls, porcelain dolls and, for the past eight to ten years, plastic dolls.

In 1980, the Contemporary Arts Center's satirical Krewe of Clones appointed twelve of New Orleans' most talented artists to design original floats for its Mardi Gras parade and ball. Lee Barnes, a noted New Orleans cooking instructor, designed and built what is probably the largest edible king cake float ever. The giant confection was pulled through the streets, cut into generous slices and distributed to merrymakers along the parade route.

Made from simple bread dough, early king cakes were not very tasty or attractive. But the king cake of today is delicious. It tastes like a coffee cake, is decorated in the Mardi Gras colors of purple, green, and gold, and is sold by virtually every bakery in town from January 6 until Mardi Gras. It would be safe to estimate that more than a half million are sold and consumed each Carnival season.

Everyone seems to be a connoisseur and to have a favorite source. Traditional cakes are available for as little as $1.50, but one can spend a small fortune to have one baked for a special function. (Those who prefer the delicacy as enjoyed in Paris will like the La Marquise Pastry Shop on Chartres Street in the French Quarter. The baker there is a native of Paris.)

On January 6 each year, the king cake tradition in New Orleans comes to life like a sleeping giant awakening with an enormous appetite. Across the city, hundreds—even thousands—of king cake parties are held daily in homes, schoolrooms, and offices, just as they were in the fourth century. The lucky person receiving the slice with the doll is crowned king and supplies the king cake for the next party.

CHAPTER EIGHT

Marching Krewes

In days gone by, few were in the financial or social position to belong to an elite Carnival krewe such as Rex, Comus, Momus, or Proteus. Today, thanks to a much larger middle class, it is estimated that over forty thousand citizens in the metropolitan New Orleans area belong to one of the many Carnival organizations.

In the nineteenth century, there was a natural longing by those with few resources to participate actively in the infectious spirit of Mardi Gras. To stand aside and merely observe those who were wealthy and fortunate enough to be direct players was not enough for some.

Neighborhood marching clubs proved to be one of the earliest ways for those without great financial means to participate in a Carnival group. Those who were unable to afford membership in the elite organizations, yet anxious to belong to a Carnival club, found marching groups economically feasible and, at the same time, as much fun (if not more).

The oldest marching club still in existence is the Jefferson City Buzzards, founded in 1889 and chartered in 1890. There are two stories about how the group got its unusual but catchy name. According to one story, the club was formed in a neighborhood known as Jefferson City that was a center for slaughterhouses and, consequently, a favorite flocking place for buzzards. Thus, members originally chose the name "Jefferson Buzzards." To eliminate confusion with neighboring Jefferson Parish, the name was changed to "Jefferson City Buzzards." The second account maintains that there was already a Carnival club in Jefferson City named the "Muddy Gras." They were great admirers of a highly successful and well-established downtown club that called itself the "French Market Buzzards." In 1889, the French Market Buzzards disbanded, and the Muddy Gras assumed the title "Jefferson City Buzzards."

The Jefferson City Buzzards were extremely shrewd about keeping costs down. Throwing small, inexpensive trinkets to the spectators had always been a highly successful part of Mardi Gras, and the Buzzards certainly wanted to keep the tradition alive. To avoid this expense and eliminate the burden of carrying heavy bags, marching club members decided instead to make colorful paper flowers and display them on tall poles. The flowers would serve yet another purpose: when a marcher spotted a pretty girl in the crowd, he would give her a flower in exchange for a kiss. One Buzzard was quoted as saying that all babies are beautiful when they're born, and all New Orleans women are beautiful on Mardi Gras. One expense the Buzzards did have to absorb was for the colorful, individually designed costumes that were different each year. The second largest expense was for a comfortable pair of walking shoes, to be painted either gold or silver.

The Buzzards are still marching today. Their typical Mardi Gras outing begins early, to get the most out of the day. At daybreak, Buzzards wearing bright costumes and carrying poles of colorful flowers meet at Tchoupitoulas Street and Audubon Park in the uptown section of the city. The first order of the day is the ritual of fortification, whereby all members partake of their favorite alcoholic beverage to chase the chill of the morning air from their bones. If the day happens to be warm and humid, this same beverage serves to keep the sweat from their brows while it cools down their bodies. This all-important fortification ritual normally takes an hour or more.

The next task is to line up in total disarray behind the purple and gilt banner that proudly proclaims that these are the antics—dancing, prancing, strutting, and every once in a while marching—of the proud and famous Jefferson City Buzzards. The band sets a jazzy pace with the syncopated rhythm of the snare drum and the sweet high notes of the trumpet. With the Buzzards all warmed up, well-fortified and anxious to do their stuff, the march gets officially under way, to the delight of the tumultuous crowds that show their appreciation by being at the starting location every year. Along the first block, every girl is given a flower and a kiss, plus an array of proudly displayed Buzzard dance steps.

The first stop of the day is made at the bar on the corner. According to the Buzzard creed, it would be un-Buzzardlike, discourteous and unthinkable to pass up a barroom on Mardi Gras. The progress of the parade is tediously slow

The St. Louis Cemetery Marching Club was short-lived.

The Jefferson City Buzzards, chartered in 1890, is the city's oldest marching club.

until the parade reaches St. Charles Avenue. Here the Buzzards go into high gear, "loose as a goose" and really ready to perform to the encouraging crowd lining the street. It is a reciprocal reaction; the more the Buzzards perform, the greater the crowd's response, and vice versa.

The Buzzards' antics last from sunrise until well after sunset. Even though they give it their best shot, some of the Buzzards never get past the fortification ritual and some only get as far as the first bar. (To put this misfortune in a positive light, at least these members won't need to make any flowers for next Mardi Gras.) Other Buzzards complete the march with sore feet and sore lips acquired by carrying out their Buzzardly duties. Of course, all the Buzzards' bodies are totally saturated with alcohol; there are countless bars between the start and finish of their march. According to Buzzard legend, one member who took part in the parade a few years ago died the day after Mardi Gras. According to his wishes, he was cremated, and his ashes burned for ninety days with little outside assistance.

It may be true that dancing, drinking and kissing come naturally to the Buzzards, but no one can say that they aren't totally dedicated to their creed of entertaining the crowds to the utmost. To stand up under the heavy demands made on their bodies the day of their march, they hold a dress rehearsal several weeks prior to Mardi Gras. That's true dedication!

Just as Comus was copied by organizations that followed, so have the Jefferson City Buzzards been imitated by various groups. There are several dozen walking clubs (including some all-female groups) active today, and dozens of others that are only memories from the past. But the Jefferson City Buzzards are still fortifying themselves and the institutions of Carnival and Mardi Gras.

A lost tradition, one of Zulu's floats was a mobile fish fry.

Instead of arriving from a distant land via the Mississippi River on a royal yacht like Rex, Zulu arrived by way of the New Basin Canal in a rowboat.

CHAPTER NINE

Zulu

With New Orleans' large black population, it was inevitable that there would be an organized black parade on Mardi Gras. History tells us that the black citizens of the city took part in Mardi Gras long before the Emancipation Proclamation of 1863. However, it was not until the twentieth century that a black krewe was organized.

In 1909, the members of a black social club called the Tramps went to see a musical comedy entitled *Smart Set* at the Pyphian Temple. A skit entitled "There Never Was and There Never Will Be a King Like Me" caught the group's attention. The Tramps liked the style and image portrayed in the skit by the African Zulu king. On the next day, the group met in a backyard across from a saloon on Perdido Street and planned the first black Mardi Gras parade. They renamed their social club the "Zulu Social Aid and Pleasure Club," and their king was to be called Zulu. The group began parading in 1910 and was officially incorporated on September 26, 1916.

The Zulu Social Aid and Pleasure Club was established more along the lines of the old New Orleans burial societies than of the other Carnival clubs. Members of the Zulus paid dues weekly. In the event of illness, they received weekly funds until they recovered; upon death, they were provided with a funeral that included a jazz band. But the main focus of the club was social. Its top priority was the enjoyment of Mardi Gras to the fullest. The Zulus thought this could be accomplished by poking a little honest fun at the white Mardi Gras monarch, Rex—the more buffoonery, the better.

The club's first year of parading, 1910, was rather bleak financially. William Story, the first Zulu king, wore a costume made from sack material that had pictures from tobacco cans and cigarette packs sewn on it. On his head, King Zulu wore a lard can that was cut into the shape of a crown. (The lard can was the type and size that could be brought to a corner barroom and filled to the brim with cold beer for five cents.) A dock worker who frequently unloaded bananas, Story carried a banana stalk as his scepter. That first year, Zulu's finances did not allow for floats, so he walked proudly, accompanied by his faithful warriors.

Every year, Rex, the King of Carnival, arrived from a faraway land on his majestic yacht by way of the mighty Mississippi River and was greeted upon arrival by a twenty-one-gun artillery salute. When Zulu's fortunes improved, he came from afar also, arriving in the city by way of the New Basin Canal in a dilapidated rowboat and being greeted upon arrival by a salute from twenty-one packs of firecrackers.

Through the years, the buffoonery and mockery continued. King Zulu's costume varied from year to year in those early days. He wore a silver foil suit made from the inner linings of cigarette packages, a rabbit skin costume, a suit sewn of different flags, and, one year, a pure white linen suit. Scepters varied from the original banana stalk to a ham bone or a loaf of Italian bread. One Zulu king was financed by his employer, a liquor distributor who sold Old Crow Whiskey; that year, Zulu walked with a broomstick and rooster.

The membership finally decided that a standard King Zulu costume should be designed for all future parades. The design chosen consisted of a grass skirt, black tights, and a wig made of moss. (The krewe's king is the mightiest king of all, the Zulu king of Africa, yet his costume includes a grass skirt from Hawaii, a wig made from moss from the swamps of Louisiana, and black tights from South Carolina!)

Zulu ultimately gave up his rowboat for a royal yacht.

ZULU

Whereas Rex krewe members wore deadpan face masks to disguise themselves, Zulu members blackened their faces and drew white rings around one eye and around the mouth. And since Rex members threw beads and trinkets from Europe and the Orient, Zulu decided to throw coconuts from South America.

Rex had numerous leadership positions in its ranks: captain, duke, parade marshal, etc. So Zulu used such leadership positions as Big Shot, Witch Doctor, Kingfish, Snake Charmer, Prognosticator, Soulful Warrior, and many others. The role of Big Shot, a position paralleling that of the Rex captain, was portrayed as a combination of a big-time New Orleans politician and an old-time Bourbon Street pimp, complete with a foot-long cigar and glass doorknobs for diamond rings and stickpins.

During the mid-1920s, Zulu chose as its queen female impersonator Alex Seymour, better known as Queen Corinne. He reigned until Mamie Williams was selected as a bona fide queen in 1933.

After overcoming early financial problems, King Zulu began a period of progress. He advanced from walking to riding a carriage, then to riding a single float, and finally to leading a full complement of floats.

The early parades were financed by selling "spots" to bar owners, who wanted Zulu to stop at their establishments with thousands of thirsty people during and after the parade. (Because of this bizarre means of financial support, the Zulu parade route was totally unpredictable until 1968, when City Ordinance 3827 required a standard route with a starting and ending time.)

In 1949, New Orleans's own Louis Armstrong, affectionately called "Satchmo" and "Dippermouth" by his many friends, agreed to be Zulu. Armstrong was born in New Orleans and raised at the Waif Boys Home. As a child, he witnessed a number of Zulu parades and later said that one of his greatest childhood dreams had been to be crowned King of the Zulus one day.

Satchmo's costume consisted of a red feathered crown, a red velvet tunic trimmed with gold sequins, black tights and gold-colored shoes. Over the tights, he wore a yellow cellophane grass skirt. Satchmo was later quoted as saying that his costume that year was what inspired Liberace's wardrobe.

Zulu stood proudly atop the king's float in his colorful costume, one hand holding his ever-present handkerchief and the other holding his horn as a scepter. His childhood dream of becoming King Zulu had come to pass, and he grinned his characteristic toothy grin. In just about every block, he played his trumpet to his heart's delight and to the delight of all who had come to see and hear him. It was easy to understand why he was known nationally as well as internationally as the world's jazz ambassador.

Louis Armstrong's popularity as Zulu was so great that after he dismounted from his throne, the entire float was dismantled piece by piece by souvenir hunters, right down to its steel frame.

In some ways, the Zulu Social Aid and Pleasure Club is still the same, but in many ways, it has changed. Gone is the lively Zulu black police force used by the organization before blacks were allowed on New Orleans's police force.

King Zulu

Gone are those spectators who second-lined (followed the parade carrying decorated umbrellas or other props and dancing to the lively music) behind the Zulu parade. Especially memorable black second-line groups were the Baby Dolls, the Golddiggers, the Zigaboos, and the Western Girls, led by Zulu's former Queen Corinne, Alex Seymour.

Gone, too, is Zulu's second float, consisting of a flat bed wagon, a wood cookstove, two men cleaning fish, and a black woman cooking it. Upon seeing a pretty girl in the crowd, King Zulu would point her out, and his warriors would carry her to his float, lifting her up to receive a hot Zulu kiss. Then he would send her to the second float for a hot mouthful of fried catfish. What more could a girl want on Mardi Gras?

Gone forever is the unpublished route of the footloose and fancy-free Zulus, who offered toasts at over fifty stops along the way to help finance the parade. Today, Zulu makes only two toasts: one at City Hall, where he toasts the mayor and other city officials, and the other at Gertrude Geddes-Willis Funeral Home, where he toasts his queen and court.

All things considered, Zulu's survival is a good example of the old formula of desire, dedication and determination combined with persistence and a positive attitude. Using this formula, the Zulus have overcome all obstacles—and history shows that there were many placed in their way.

One of these obstacles was internal strife, the poison that destroys many clubs. After World War II, only a handful of hardcore Zulus kept the organization from disbanding. In 1947, the president of the Mobile Colored Carnival

Gone are the lively groups who followed the Zulu parade.

ZULU

Association severely chastised the Zulus for the image they were supposedly portraying of a proud race. After this came Ordinance No. 3827, stating that no club would be issued a parade permit until a route with a time schedule for all stops was filed with the city. Many felt that the ordinance was designed specifically to destroy the Zulu organization.

With the coming of the civil rights movement, Zulu had to go against the powerful NAACP, which collected twenty-eight thousand signatures on a petition to boycott the Zulu parade and published the list of signatures in the press. (Members had the same complaints as the Mobile group.) Zulu members' businesses were also threatened with boycott.

Because of pressure exerted in 1961, the Zulu king and queen resigned. The Zulus wanted to cancel the parade, but a visit to the group by the mayor of the city and the superintendent of police convinced them that it would be in their best interests to parade. The city guaranteed full protection from any hostile elements, and Zulu did parade in spite of threats. A member agreed to serve as king that year, but his identity (for good reason) was never revealed. Zulu's problems continued in 1966 when a fire mysteriously destroyed all the organization's floats.

Men with less character would have given up long ago, but the men who run the Zulu Social Aid and Pleasure Club are no doubt men who have deep courage of conviction. No city ordinances, social do-gooders, fire bombings, or infiltrations of their ranks by those who joined to try to destroy the organization would succeed. The Zulu organization showed that it had the right stuff to survive.

King Zulu has been the humblest of all Mardi Gras kings. When he could not afford to come to the city on a royal yacht, he came in a rowboat by way of the New Basin Canal. When he could not afford a float, he walked. When he had no fancy costume as the other monarchs had, he fashioned one of sack material and cigarette packs and crafted his crown from a lard can. The theme of the Zulus, "There Never Was and There Never Will Be a King Like Me" fits the king to a *t*.

The Zulu Social Aid and Pleasure Club's main purpose is to have fun. One of its principal forms of fun is to satirize the King of Carnival; therefore, in New Orleans vernacular, one might say that King Zulu is truly the "Clown Prince of Mardi Gras."

A winning truck of the Elks Krewe.

CHAPTER TEN

Truck Krewes

To some, being only a spectator in the colorful Carnival production is not enough. The proliferation of new organizations indicates the dedication with which merrymakers seek to become official members of the cast of organized participants. For those interested in making the leap from watching to being watched, there is usually a slot to fit the means.

As early as the nineteenth century, people decorated carriages, wagons, milk carts and other rolling stock, donned costumes, and—with liquid refreshments and food to sustain them for the day—headed for the crowded streets to join fellow revelers.

The year 1933 was a bleak one for the citizens of New Orleans. Like most Americans, New Orleanians were suffering from the effects of the Great Depression, which followed the stock market crash of 1929. So the approach of Mardi Gras that year filled the city with great anticipation. Perhaps it would get people's minds off the unpleasant conditions, if only for a day.

Because of the economic situation, Momus and Proteus were forced to cancel their parades, but Rex was scheduled to roll as usual. However, as fate would have it, Rex had to be cancelled because of rain, the only time in its illustrious 111 years that the Rex parade has been cancelled because of the weather.

A young man named Chris R. Valley, who belonged to the Benevolent and Protective Order of Elks, Lodge No. 30, worked with other young members of the club until 4:00 on that Mardi Gras morning. They were getting their truck decorated for their traditional trek—roaming whatever streets they could find passable (trucks were not allowed on the parade routes), dancing in the streets, visiting friends and relatives, and ending up at one of several parks to eat, drink, and generally have a good time.

When the early morning downpour that had forced Rex to cancel ended around noon, the seventy masked riders of the Elks group mounted their forty-foot trailer truck and took to the streets with a four-piece band. The theme of their decorations was "The White Indians." Other groups who had spent a great deal of energy (and little money) readying their trucks did likewise. So although the people of New Orleans failed to see a Rex parade in 1933, they did enjoy an array of colorfully decorated trucks with more costumed riders than they had ever seen in any Mardi Gras procession.

That Mardi Gras, Valley thought of Mildred Washburn, the editor of his school newspaper and a very imaginative lady who had successfully organized truck parades for the students. These parades were successful, but she had never fulfilled her lifelong dream of sneaking a truck onto the parade route to follow Rex. Thus the idea of organizing all of the Elks trucks into one cohesive, fun-loving group was born. Here was a chance to fulfill Mildred Washburn's dream for her.

Valley studied every aspect of such a revolutionary undertaking, and after another dry run in 1934, he presented his idea to fellow Elks members. The date was September 6, 1934. The Elks received and approved the idea of a truck parade with great enthusiasm. As quickly as they could arrange an appointment, Valley and a group of Elks went to City Hall and presented the idea to city officials, who were impressed enough to give Lodge No. 30 of the Benevolent and Protective Order of Elks a permit to follow Rex down the traditional route on Mardi Gras 1935.

One of the many virtues of the Elks organization is charity; therefore, it was decided that the king and queen of the Elks truck parade would be selected from a local orphanage rather than from the membership. This would allow less-fortunate children to be royalty for a day.

The first truck parade was well-received by the 1935 Mardi Gras crowd and has grown every year since. It is now made up of 150 trucks with an average of 40 people per vehicle—a total of 6,000 enthusiastic masked riders throwing to an equally enthusiastic, appreciative crowd. There is a waiting list of prospective participants. In 1981, there were 181 trucks with an average of forty people per truck, or 7,240 riders, but the city decided that a limit of 150 trucks in the Elks parade was enough. The Crescent City truck ensemble follows the 150-truck Elks convoy, and it was considered unfair to Crescent City to add more and more trucks in front of it every year.

In all, there are five truck parades on Mardi Gras: Elks Krewe of Orleanians (the krewe name adopted by the city's Elks) and Crescent City in Orleans Parish; the Krewe of Jefferson and Elks Krewe of Jeffersonians in Jefferson Parish; and the Krewe of St. Bernard in St. Bernard Parish.

There is also one unofficial truck parade in New Orleans, the Krewe of Tucks, made up mostly of students from fraternities and sororities of the uptown universities and colleges of Tulane, Loyola, St. Mary's Dominican, and Newcomb. Originally, they rode only trucks, but have now added traditional, standard-size floats to their parade. The Krewe of Tucks, like all Mardi Gras krewes, is truly a fun-loving group. Its motto, as depicted on its doubloon, is "booze, beer, bourbon, and broads."

In the five official truck krewes combined, there are an estimated eighteen thousand costumed riders who know how to have a good time. All five award

Organized truck parades did not roll until the first Elks Krewe of Orleanians followed Rex in 1935, but the use of decorated trucks goes back to the early 1900s.

trophies for the best decorated trucks and, as special recognition, the winners are placed in the lead spot in the next parade. Other awards presented are for best headdress, best costume, and most unique theme.

The top winner in the Elks Krewe of Orleanians is presented the coveted Chris Valley grand-prize trophy, named in honor of the man who had the vision and the drive to put into motion a truck extravaganza that merits the title "world's longest parade."

Just prior to midnight on Mardi Gras, the krewes of Rex and Comus meet. Rex and Comus escort each other's queens in a grand march. Rex then waves his scepter, and Mardi Gras is officially over for another year.

CHAPTER ELEVEN

End of Mardi Gras, Beginning of Lent

According to an old saying, all roads lead to Rome. On Mardi Gras, all roam the roads that lead to parade routes.

According to another old saying, all good things must come to an end.

The long Carnival season, which officially begins on January 6 with the ball of the Twelfth Night Revelers, ends at the stroke of midnight on Mardi Gras. Sandwiched in between those two dates are almost one hundred magnificent Mardi Gras balls and some sixty street parades, where millions of doubloons and other trinkets are thrown to the outstretched hands of unbelievably well-behaved crowds. In 1983, twelve of these sixty parades were held on Mardi Gras.

As a warm-up on the big day (as if one is needed), before the main attractions of Rex, Zulu, Argus, and others come the colorful walking clubs with their flowers, kisses, and prancing, dancing antics. And after the major float parades come the hundreds of decorated truck floats carrying thousands of maskers.

The last official parade is that of Comus, the oldest krewe. With tradition a high priority, Comus floats are still illuminated by colorful flambeaux as they were in 1857. The same deadpan masks worn then are worn now.

Comus is the god of joy and mirth, not a king. He wears a headdress of white plumes instead of a crown and carries a golden goblet instead of a scepter.

When the Krewe of Comus reaches Canal Street, the god's float stops in front of the Boston Club, where Comus offers a toast to Rex, the official King of Carnival.

Just as in 1857, the Krewe of Comus goes on to hold its ball immediately after its nighttime parade. Right before midnight, when the tableau is completed, Rex—who is reigning over his own ball in the other half of the same auditorium—arrives at the Comus ball with his queen and their court to join Comus and his queen and court. Upon entering, Rex bows to Comus, and the two change partners for a grand march around the auditorium floor.

On Ash Wednesday, a priest makes a cross of ashes on a Christian worshiper's forehead while saying, "Remember, man, from dust thou came and to dust thou shall return."

At exactly midnight, the four stop. Rex waves his scepter to his royal subjects. On that signal, Mardi Gras is officially over for another year.

All that merriment spread over all those weeks makes the original Christian purpose of Mardi Gras easy to overlook. Fat Tuesday was instituted to allow Christians to fatten up before Lenten fasting and abstinence. As early as the fourth century, fasting as penance was an official precept of the Church in Rome and spread quickly to other Christian countries.

On Ash Wednesday, many Catholics stand before a priest who marks the sign of the cross on each worshipper's forehead with ashes made by burning the palms from the previous Palm Sunday's services. As the cross is made, the clergyman says, "Remember, man, from dust thou came and to dust thou shall return." A sobering thought indeed after weeks of physical license.

Afterword

Since the first Mardi Gras celebration in Louisiana was held on the banks of the Mississippi in 1699, the observance has grown to the extent that New Orleans is now, without challenge, the Mardi Gras capital of the world.

Until the mid-1850s, there were no Mardi Gras parades. New Orleans was located on land below sea level and lacked adequate drainage; muddy streets were not conducive to heavy foot traffic, so individual, unorganized masking and Mardi Gras dances were the only forms of celebration. With the birth of the Krewe of Comus in 1857 came the first organized parade, complete with floats, flambeaux, masked riders, and a leading citizen to serve as Comus. The procession was followed by a ball with four tableaux for the enjoyment of three thousand selected guests. Comus thus instituted the first of many changes in the annual celebration.

Whether a full-fledged parading group with a ball like Comus or simply a modest marching group or truck krewe, each new organization has contributed fresh ideas. The Civil War and World Wars I and II retarded progress but, following these calamities, the celebration grew tremendously. After World War II, Carnival experienced its greatest increase in the number of krewes ever in one decade: twenty-five were added, with each contributing nuances of its own. In the '50s, fourteen new organizations were formed; in the '60s, sixteen. That's a total of fifty-five in thirty years.

Among those founded in the '60s was Bacchus, which in 1968 initiated massive fundamental changes that would prove to have invigorating effects on the celebration as a whole. All previous krewes had catered primarily to the people of the general metropolitan area, but Bacchus's aim was to cater to out-of-town visitors as well.

What Bacchus proposed was designed to bring national and international attention to New Orleans and, at the same time, add to the enjoyment of the locals. The revolutionary new krewe built larger, more elaborate floats that would hold more riders. Membership was open to a wide range of people in the business and professional community. In place of a traditional ball with invitations sent to a tight list of select guests, the group held a huge dinner dance at the Rivergate Convention Center for its members and their guests, thereby reflecting the wider participation of the original Carnival balls. To add splendor to the occasion, the floats were brought into the Rivergate to serve as a backdrop for those attending the function.

To attract more international interest, the krewe chose a nationally known celebrity for its king instead of selecting a member of the krewe or a leading citizen of the community. It was a move that would later be followed by several other krewes.

Bacchus's innovations in '68 were departures as drastic as were the first ball and parade organized by Comus in 1857. If there is one element that is constant in Carnival and Mardi Gras, it is change, and Bacchus has brought about a full measure. However, despite the marked change, the members who were there at the beginning will tell you that there was no concerted attempt to break tradition, only to give the existing structure of the celebration a lift. If tradition was altered, the alteration simply happened as a by-product of the original goal of attracting wider interest.

Part 2

BACCHUS
Introduction to Part 2

Seems like only yesterday when a few brazen souls banded together to launch what would become a major catalyst to Carnival as we had known it in New Orleans. It was 1968.

In the two dozen years since the end of World War II, our city had evolved from a sleepy riverside community to a thriving Southern commercial center. Skyscrapers would soon stalk the skyline as proof of an upward economic surge.

And yet, there were problems surfacing in the infrastructure of our city. Brought about in part by aging alone, the challenges would require massive infusions of capital . . . ours and others'.

Tourism, the lagniappe industry, appeared to be faltering, or at least not growing as it should have been. One big center of attraction—Mardi Gras—had grown a little stale in the eyes of the shakers and movers. The entrenched exclusivity of the inner workings of the celebration would no longer be accepted by a more educated, better informed, more discerning populace.

Recognizing the need for something new, visionary Owen Brennan, Sr., had long fancied a Carnival krewe that would open doors to wider participation— for its membership as well as for the man, woman and child on the street. His son Owen, Jr., and brother Dick picked up on the idea and called a meeting of "young turks." I was privileged to be among that group, along with Harold Spaid, Larry Youngblood, Pete Moss, Marshall Pearce, Doug Regan, Bob Sonfield, Jim Nassikas, Ted Dampeer and Carl Smith, Jr.

Actually, we were too naive to appreciate the enormity of the enterprise we were undertaking. We didn't know it couldn't or shouldn't be done, so we did it.

MARDI GRAS AND BACCHUS

We began the organization of the Krewe of Bacchus. It was not our intention to compete with or break tradition. We wanted to add something, to give a boost to Carnival and Mardi Gras as they were. A celebrity king, we thought, would be our best vehicle.

Today, judging from the size of the parade crowds, the eventual response of old-line krewes, the local, regional and national media coverage, and the growth of our membership, just about everyone seems to be pleased that we did it.

Look around at the floats of most krewes compared with pre-1969, when the Bacchus parade first rolled. Look at the public's reaction to the Carnival season and Mardi Gras Day. What was an off-night (the Sunday before Fat Tuesday) has now become an event second, perhaps, only to Mardi Gras Day. And what a fitting prelude Bacchus has become!

Look around at the national personalities donating their time to New Orleans, to the celebration, to the parade. They have come here to help give the people on the street "the greatest free show on earth." In its first six years,* Bacchus crowned Danny Kaye, Raymond Burr, Jim Nabors, Phil Harris, Bob Hope, and Glen Campbell—every one a giant in the entertainment industry.

Since the reign of Glen Campbell, nine more years have come and gone, and the krewe continues to improve its spectacular. Floats get better, crowds grow larger, other krewes become stronger. And the lagniappe industry thrives. A sluggish infrastructure is now being revitalized to meet our needs in the twenty-first century.

I believe the addition of Bacchus to Carnival and Mardi Gras has played a small but important role in restoring a measure of vitality and sparkle to the jewel on the Mississippi.

From small acorns do large oaks grow; from bold ideas do changes flow. Anti-tradition, even when it's accidental, eventually becomes tradition, for Bacchus and for Carnival as a whole.

AUGUST PEREZ III
Bacchus Captain

*The first six years of Bacchus are featured in the book Bacchus by Myron Tassin, published in 1975 by Pelican Publishing Company.

CHAPTER TWELVE

Bacchus VII, 1975
How Sweet It Wasn't

The statement that Jackie Gleason is a giant in the entertainment business can be interpreted in different ways. In this case, the description is intended to mean "great" instead of "large."

Likewise, the statement that the Krewe of Bacchus is a roaring success will generate varying responses from each person who hears it. Some enjoy Bacchus because of the vast sea of humanity it attracts on the Sunday before Mardi Gras; to others, the huge floats are the attraction. Still others like Bacchus because of its generous riders and high-quality throws. Some like Bacchus because the krewe has flaunted change in a city built on tradition. To the fan who sees the big picture, Bacchus is all of the above and more.

Nevertheless, without the celebrity king,* Bacchus would not be the catalytic converter it has grown to be—filtering out the old exclusivity of the Carnival season and giving the general public and tourists a measure of participatory air to breathe. The king is central, and every spectator becomes a critic: "Bob Hope was the best." "Me, I liked Phil Harris; he was loaded." "The children liked Danny Kaye so much." "Jim Nabors fell in love with New Orleans and has continued to participate in Bacchus." And on and on it goes.

Gleason came with all the credentials to be Bacchus VII. In fact, when he donned his robes, one of the krewe members remarked that he looked like Henry VIII. Like Hope and Harris, Kaye and Campbell, Nabors and Burr, Gleason had been a part of America's living rooms and dens for years—first as Chester A. Riley, then as Ralph Kramden, and later with his star-studded variety show. "The Honeymooners" has become a television classic. Millions watch the reruns as Ralph and Norton continue to endear themselves to their fans with predictable buffoonery. "And away we go" and "How sweet it is" have become household expressions to rival "I kid you not" and "I don't get no respect."

*The Krewe of Bacchus was named after the god of wine; therefore, it is not altogether proper to use the term "king" when referring to the person serving as Bacchus. However, popular and media usage of such terms as "king of Bacchus" and "celebrity king" have established "king" as part of the local vernacular.

Gleason with pages

At a dinner party at Brennan's the night before Bacchus Sunday, Gleason said he had been given ample preparation by former Bacchus king Bob Hope. In fact, Gleason had left after fifteen holes of Hope's golf classic that Saturday afternoon to make the trip to New Orleans, where he was received with a brass band. "Between Hope and Phil Harris, I've heard all about Bacchus, and I can't wait until tomorrow night," the rotund comedian said as he relished the horseradish in the shrimp remoulade.

On Sunday evening, however, much to the consternation of his subjects, it became apparent that King Gleason had left Ralph Kramden behind. He came instead as a gentle, polite, almost withdrawn man entering a kingdom of loud, boisterous crazies; they looked for the clown, but found a person quite different from the parts he had portrayed on the television screen. He was typecast, but wouldn't play the role.

The critics were not pleased. Bacchus members were not amused. Later, when asked in a survey to name their favorite king, "The Great One" did not receive many votes. True, the king-for-a-night toasted Mayor Moon Landrieu and other dignitaries at Gallier Hall and perfunctorily announced how sweet it was. But Joe and Jane Public, accustomed to the likes of Phil Harris, were not impressed, as Gleason appeared to be bored by the whole mindless mania.

(Charter member Tony Fasola likes to recount the year Phil Harris rode as a past king. "He was so elated, [he] got smashed and passed out on the front of the float. Krewe members immediately covered his body in total with beads and doubloons so he could not be seen. Then, in front of City Hall, he arose like Godzilla from beneath the doubloons and, of course, the tuxedos and evening dresses went wild. . . . [The Bacchanals wearing them] thought this was part of the act. Fantastic! Then Phil asked, 'What time does the parade start?' ")

"Gleason simply didn't get with it" was the overriding comment. At the Rendezvous following the parade, he appeared anxious to get back to the privacy of his hotel room, and left the Rivergate for his Royal Orleans suite long before the supper dance was in full swing.

A later king, Henry Winkler, would make a point of emphasizing that he had left his character, the Fonz, behind—that this was *his* night. Still, he was very

Riding lieutenants clasp hands with Gleason

entertaining, he was eager to please, and he got into the spirit of the moment. Although out of character, he was one of Bacchus' most popular kings.

Bacchus photographer Ralph Romaguera remembered Gleason in this manner: "He never seemed very enthused" and was "quite grumpy all night." Gleason seemed unable to appreciate the idea that Carnival is letting loose, letting go, a last fling.

However, if the subjects didn't fully appreciate their ruler, the parade made up for the turn-off in spades. Besides the usual beads and doubloons, Bacchus members threw attractive necklaces for the first time. The crowd, estimated to be the largest up to that point for the young organization's parade, responded joyously with walls of waving arms and hands.

Paying tribute to the animals and entertainers who have long thrilled circus audiences, the theme of the parade was "Bacchus's Circus Parade." Highlighting the marchers were the Olympia Brass Band and eighteen high school and college ensembles. The humongous Budweiser Clydesdales pulled their colorful wagon.

The parade route took twenty-three massive floats from a starting point on Louisiana Avenue down St. Charles Avenue to Canal Street, up Canal to Claiborne Avenue, and back down Canal to the Rivergate where the Rendezvous was held.

Floats included (in order of appearance): the officers of the krewe, with the giant figure of Bacchus "in his cups" grinning wildly; the king of Bacchus in his royal robes; the title float; "Circus Clowns"; circus figure P. T. Barnum holding Tom Thumb, the world's smallest man; "Lions and Tigers"; "Monkeys and Giraffes"; "The Side Show"; "Jumbo the Elephant"; "Acrobats"; the familiar reptilian wino, "Bacchusaurus"; "Trained Seal Act"; "Jugglers, Dancing Bears, The Human Cannonball"; "High-Flying Aerialists"; "Bareback Riders"; perennial favorites "King Kong" and "Queen Kong"; "The Concession Stand"; "The Great Magician Act"; "Belly Dancers"; and "The Calliope."

Early on Ash Wednesday morning, as weary revelers found their pillows after days and weeks of spirited partying, they knew they had again been to the largest annual outdoor party in the world. And Jackie Gleason probably didn't yet fully understand what had occurred.

BACCHUS IN COLOR

Jackie Gleason

Perry Como at Rivergate

Henry Winkler at Rivergate

Tom Bosley, Winkler, Howard and Donny Most at Rivergate

King Kong

"Circus Parade," title float during Gleason's reign

Pete Fountain toasting the people

Float entering Rivergate during Winkler's reign

Ed McMahon at Gallier Hall

Float during McMahon's reign

DeLuise second-lining with his mother

Winkler dancing with
Southern University coed

Dom DeLuise addresses his subjects at Rivergate

Portrait of a ruler: Charlton Heston

Sgt. John McKeel throwing first doubloons

Fountain on stage at Rivergate

Bacchusaurus

Heston and wife partying, New Orleans style

CHAPTER THIRTEEN

Bacchus VIII, 1976
Perry Como—
It's Impossible

Of all the celebrity kings he's known, float lieutenant Milton Retif liked Perry Como best. You could tell Como had "strong feelings for the crowds [and] individuals," he said.

That statement might just about summarize the feelings of television viewers who had admired and loved Como since his rise to stardom. He seemed to truly "love those dear hearts and gentle people" of New Orleans. The "Mr. Nice Guy" image came across just as it had on the tube in homes across America.

Those who had the pleasure of his company during his stay in New Orleans will tell you he's a toucher, a smiler. Of course, this might be a result of his Mediterranean heritage; but the easygoing, low-key image seems real nonetheless. Board member Tony Brocato maintains that Como "was the easiest [of all the kings] to work with."

Como told a reporter that in television, you're going into people's living rooms and they don't like for you to push. He emphasized that you can't be on the air all those years and not enjoy it or enjoy people.

Proof of the pudding was his demeanor during the week preceding Bacchus as he worked on the taping of one of his on-location specials. The handsome, graying sixty-three-year-old (at the time) performer was the epitome of control. Although his efficient, professional staff kept things moving as smoothly as one can expect a beehive to run, it was Como who made the big decisions. When he wasn't directly involved, he would leave the set to relax.

The star did become a little miffed when some of his crew members complained about sound clutter in the background. To Como, that was part of doing a show on location. He could have lip-synched to a pre-recorded number, but refused, explaining that he rarely sings a song the same way twice. It depends on his mood and the mind-set of his audience.

An observer could tell that he had not been corrupted or made cynical by Hollywood. Married for forty-three years and the grandparents of many, Como

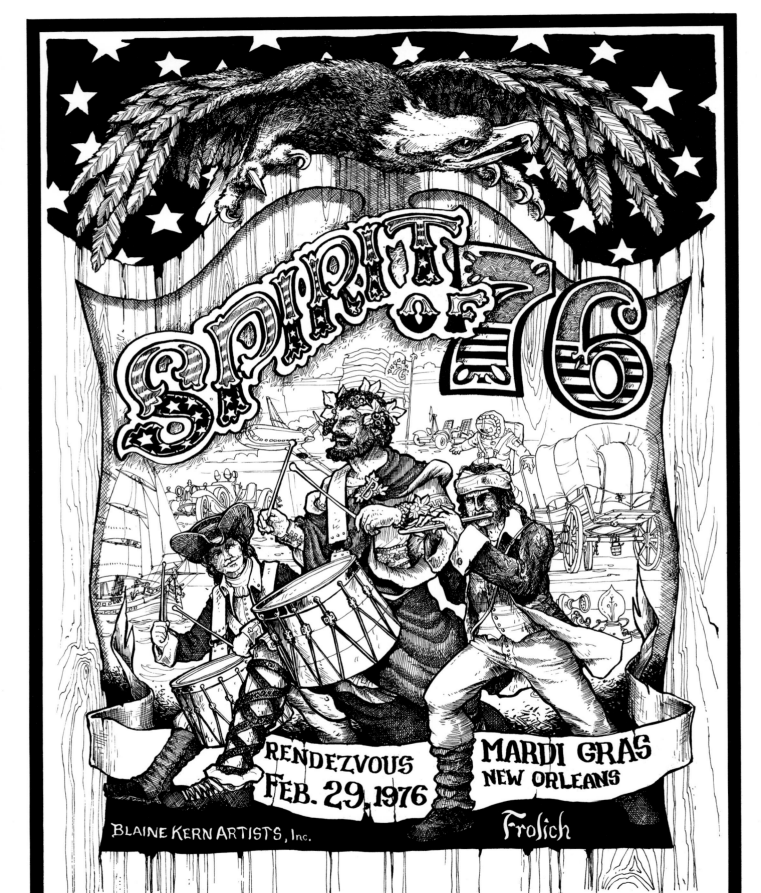

and his wife, Roselle, preferred to live in Florida, so they had never stayed in California for any length of time. Hollywood never really knew Como, and he apparently had little interest in knowing Hollywood.

Como allowed that he didn't like the movies he had been thrown into, because he didn't think they made much sense. He must have forgotten where he was when he mentioned, as an example of his more unrealistic roles, the part he once played of a singer running for governor. What about Louisiana's singing governor, Jimmie Davis, Mr. C.?

Although film may not have been his medium, he demonstrated clearly that television was as he strolled on and off the set—adjusting, adapting, and relaxing the hard-working guests, among whom were Dick Van Dyke and Leslie Uggams.

When it came time to outfit the crooner for his Bacchus robes, Como asked how long he would be in the lavish garb. Told that it would be seven or eight hours, he respectfully requested a little larger neck size. The grand attire would suit him well for his triumphant procession through the city and its fun-loving people.

It was 1976—the Bicentennial of the United States—so the progressive Bacchus krewe was eager to maintain its reputation for the unexpected splash. If Carnival and Mardi Gras can present the largest outdoor party in the world, why not have the largest indoor party, too? So it was announced that there would be a party for the public in the Superdome on Bacchus night between 6:00 P.M. and 2:00 A.M. The party would include an all-star lineup of performers, including local favorites Ronnie Kole and Lou Sino, the Ike and Tina Turner Review, the Southern University Band, and the Harry James Orchestra. As a special attraction, the parade itself, with the theme "Bacchus Presents—The Spirit of '76," would enter the giant flying-saucer-like Dome and parade around its field for the enjoyment of the partying thousands. It was a new wrinkle for the unpredictable krewe.

The parade began and ended at the Rivergate. It traveled up Poydras Street to St. Charles Avenue, then went around Lee Circle, up Howard Avenue to Loyola Avenue and northwest to and through the Superdome, where a crowd of twenty thousand reviewed in comfort.

It was 9:30 P.M. before the mobile display left the Dome for Poydras Street, wound down to St. Charles and northeast to Canal, went up Canal to Claiborne, and then traveled back down Canal to the Rivergate.

The snaking, looping, five-hour-long trek through the downtown business district allowed some paradegoers to see the pageantry two or three times. And the distance made the Bacchus king thankful that he had asked for a loose collar.

Downtown New Orleans could have been just another living room as Como fans, especially the over-forty crowd, lavished adulation upon their longtime friend. "Hey, Perry dawlin'—I luv ya." "Gawd, doll, he sure looks good." "Where y'at, Per, hon?" For once, Governor Edwin Edwards—a surprise, unmasked guest on one of the floats—was not the center of attention. Nor did he try to be.

Como, friends, and pages

To the quiet, easygoing Como, the mad scene on Canal might have reminded him of one of his songs, "It's Impossible." But he was quickly coming to realize that in New Orleans, everything is possible. Photographer Ralph Romaguera thought Como was a "very nice fella." "His agent seemed very nervous because of the Al Hirt publicity a few years before," Romaguera remembers. "Once he [Como] got into the spirit, he was very loose and enjoyed himself."

Around 11:00 P.M., the first of the twenty-four floats began to enter the Rivergate like lazy inchworms, to be met by an impatient crowd of diners and dancers. The mammoth floats were as follows, in order: the parade marshal's float, king's float, Bacchus officers, theme float, "Spirit of Exploration," "Spirit of Friendship," "Spirit of Liberty," "Spirit of Courage," "Spirit of Expansion," "Spirit of Victory," "Spirit of Invention," "Spirit of Tranquility," "Spirit of Expression," "Spirit of Competition," "Spirit of Music," "Spirit of Brotherhood," "Spirit of Hope," "King Kong," "Queen Kong," "Bacchusaurus," and "God Bless America Spirit."

The roof of the Rivergate must have expanded slightly to accommodate all the cheering and applause. As King Como left the king's float and inched his way to the stage, people followed to touch a sleeve or try to make eye contact, as if proximity might confirm his existence. Como proceeded to make a few remarks on the magnitude of it all—in size and in emotion. He sang a few favorite songs and met many of his subjects.

The celebrity king had been celebrated. Mr. C had been to see for himself.

Como, friends

CHAPTER FOURTEEN

Bacchus IX, 1977 King Henry

In its annual search for a king, the krewe naturally hopes its selection will meet the approval of Bacchus members. However, the prime consideration is the public's enjoyment.

In 1976, Perry Como had appealed to those in their middle and upper years; in 1977, it was hoped that the king would appeal primarily to the younger set. But Bacchus IX, Henry Winkler, star of ABC-TV's "Happy Days," quickly transcended the generation gap. And, as lagniappe, he won the admiration of krewe members as well. Later, he would be voted one of their favorite kings. Aaaaay!

On December 18, 1976, in a clever publicity stunt, Winkler willingly agreed to talk by phone from Hollywood to five children at Bissonet Plaza School in Metairie (a New Orleans suburb) who were celebrating their birthdays that month. Winkler told them that he had been waiting twenty years to get back to New Orleans, "but to come back as a major part of Mardi Gras is a pleasure I cannot adequately convey to you." He explained that he could not say "no" to the Bacchus invitation.

At the youngsters' request, Winkler did something he refuses to do except on "Happy Days"—utter his famous Fonz exclamation, "Aaaaay!" When asked if it was true that he was afraid of liver, he said that the Fonz doesn't like liver, but Henry Winkler does.

The king-to-be spoke fondly of his sister and of reading, and then closed with "Happy Birthday." It would be a phone call to remember for the five young people.

Winkler's public approval rating continued to zoom when he arrived at New Orleans International Airport. It was a Saturday, the day before Bacchus Sunday. His fans had begun to gather shortly after noon, even though their hero wasn't due in until around 4:00. The group was mostly teenagers, but there was also a considerable contingent of ladies in their twenties, thirties, and forties. Support from that segment seemed a sure thing.

BACCHUS IX

The large crowd, a brass band, and krewe members throwing doubloons led Bacchus IX to call his reception "the most incredible thing I have ever seen." Obviously, the popular "Happy Days" hero had experienced his share of unusual entrances, but this was something special.

Winkler's parents were on hand as guests of the krewe, and when he saw his mother, he excused himself and went over to greet her, quipping, "I know this lady; she follows me everywhere."

Following the family reunion, Winkler was ushered ever so slowly through jammed corridors to an airport suite for a noisy, upbeat press conference. The television star spoke candidly, emphasizing from the beginning that he had left the Fonz and his leather jacket in California. He made it clear that Winkler the man, not Fonzie the character, would be Bacchus IX.

"Just call me King Henry," he decreed. And to demonstrate his power, he proceeded to cancel all taxes.

Ed Nelson playing Harry Truman

In a serious vein, Winkler contended he is nothing like the brash, tough, confident Fonz in private life, and professed a fear of motorcycles and an aversion to ducktail hair cuts. (His yearning to escape the mold would be for naught on Sunday night; the fifties music selected for the Superdome Extravaganza would leave no doubt as to the identity of the king or his television role.)

The Yale graduate was as well-spoken as he was soft-spoken. And it was plain to see that he was profoundly honored to be the krewe's selection. His father, a German lumberman, joshed about his failure to attract his son into the business. But he admitted admiration for Henry's meteoric rise to stardom. After just three years of "Happy Days," the television giant had already amassed a soaring following.

Mrs. Winkler insisted that she always knew her son would be a performer. "Since he was a little boy, he always wanted to act," she told reporters, "but I didn't think it would lead to this."

As he left the press conference, he was greeted by yelling, adoring fans—a capsule preview of things to come.

At the pre-parade suiting-up party the next afternoon, it became apparent that Bacchus IX would be as popular with krewe members as he was with the public. M. L. Lagarde, a longtime Bacchus member, recalls, "He got into the swing of things and was extremely friendly toward the entire krewe." And the instant rapport between monarch and his subjects carried over to the streets from the very beginning of the parade.

The procession left the Rivergate and moved up Poydras, turned away from the downtown area along St. Charles to a turnaround at Washington Avenue. It then went back up St. Charles to Lee Circle, up Howard to Loyola, and up Girod Street to and through the Superdome. On leaving the Dome party, the march of gargantuan floats traveled down Poydras to Loyola, along Loyola to Canal and toward the Mississippi River for its destination, the Rivergate.

Krewe member Dennis Brisolara recalls Winkler's initial reaction upon leaving the Rivergate: "Watching his enthusiasm at the start of the parade showed that no matter how popular or large the star, the kings are in awe of the people instead of the people in awe of the kings." Brisolara's thesis was clearly evident as the surging river of people slowed the king's float to a crawl.

Winkler stands on throne

Ernest Borgnine and friends

Meanwhile, the second Superdome Extravaganza was in full swing on what might have been called "rock 'n' roll night." The show included such immortal performers from the fifties as Chuck Berry and Bo Diddley as well as local favorites Vince Vance and the Valiants. Old men "rocked" with young girls, and young boys "rolled" with their mothers. It was Carnival of the Bacchus variety, where age has no bounds and class has no place.

Ed Nelson introduces Benji to Winkler

Looking sharp

BACCHUS IX

After police cleared a path through the swarm of revelers buzzing on the arena floor, the parade rolled into the mammoth structure to thunderous applause. The piercing screams of breathless girls were deafening: "Throw me something, Fonz!" Buckets of doubloons and thousands of strained vocal cords later, an incredulous but smiling and responding Bacchus IX departed on the lead float to greet the avalanche of humanity awaiting his arrival on the thoroughfare known as Canal Street.

Bacchus officers followed on the second float, and next came the theme float, "Happily Ever After." The familiar "Bacchusaurus" was joined by a series of floats that reminded viewers of old-fashioned children's literature with happy endings: "Aesop's Fables," "Treasure Island," "Jack and the Beanstalk," "Sleeping Beauty," "Frog Prince," "Mother Goose," "1001 Nights," "Cinderella," "Peter Pan," "Tom Thumb," "Snow White," "Hansel and Gretel," "King Midas," "Pinocchio," "Wizard of Oz," "Little Red Riding Hood," and "Aladdin and His Wonderful Lamp."

It was a love affair between Bacchus IX and the crowd throughout the extraordinary procession. Riding lieutenant Larry McMillan's mount gave him the vantage point and maneuverability to observe and compare Winkler's reception with that of past kings. McMillan said Winkler had crowd appeal; "Others were better for the membership" in his opinion, but King Henry was a tremendous crowd pleaser.

Float lieutenant Milton Retif agreed: "His youth and enthusiasm seemed to excite the crowd." Edmond Montaldo added another positive comment: "He related to the crowd better than [any] other Bacchus." George Gaudin also felt Winkler had his finger on the pulse of the crowd: "He was a very happy man and looked as if he enjoyed himself thoroughly."

One member, float lieutenant Paul Skretny, disagreed with those who had been concerned that Winkler would appeal only to young people. "He sincerely enjoyed himself as king and conveyed that feeling to everyone," Skretny maintained. "He appealed to all ages."

Winkler was Albert Luke, Jr.'s favorite king because of "his outward, total enthusiasm." Rider Marshall Davis, son of member L. B. Davis, Jr., felt the enthusiastic monarch "seemed to enjoy being king more than most . . . he never dreamed things like this went on in New Orleans."

Ralph Romaguera saw Winkler from a special viewpoint—behind a camera—and judged him one of Bacchus's best kings.

When Bacchus IX entered the Rivergate, he seemed to be transfixed. The touching reception from New Orleanians had been an experience fit for a king. (Aaaay, King Fonz, what did you expect? A hot dog at Arnold's Drive-In with Richie?) But before long, the king came down to earth and went to work—or was it play?—entertaining krewe members and their guests.

Hours later, on the way back to his hotel, the dethroned ruler saw the sanitation crews collecting the tons of debris left by the bacchanals during the parade. The multitudes were gone—from Canal Street, but not from Henry Winkler's mind. The memories of that night would stay with him forever. And he would be back to see it all again—sooner than he imagined.

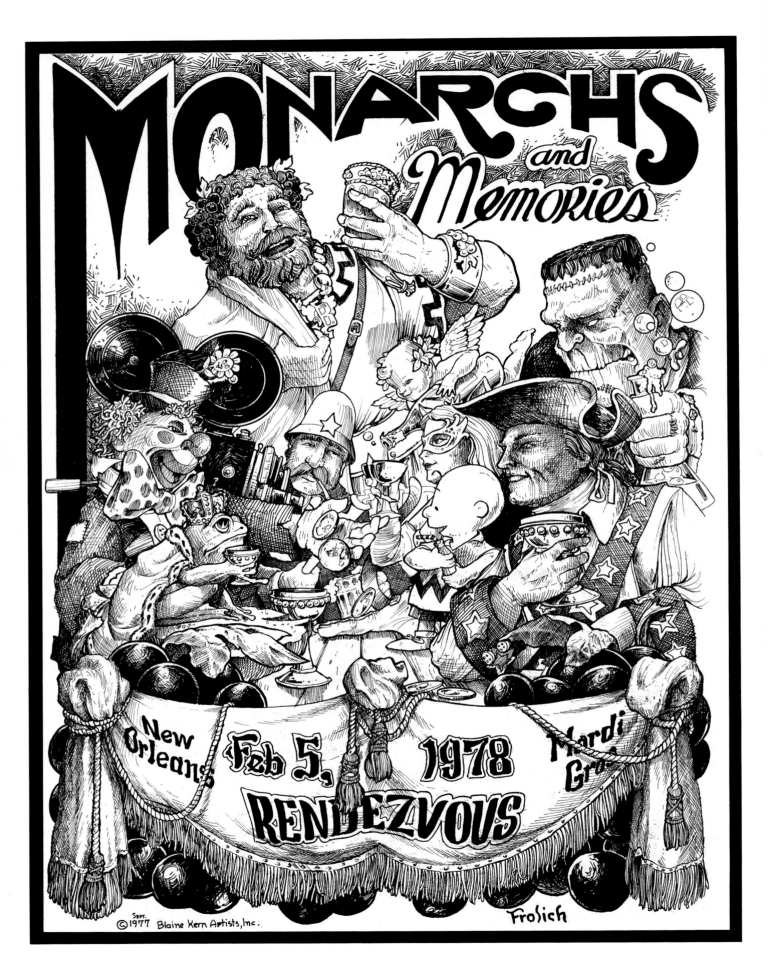

CHAPTER FIFTEEN

Bacchus X, 1978
Her-r-re's Bacchus

Ever notice how "The Tonight Show" is not quite the same when Ed McMahon is out of town? Doc Severinsen does a decent job of filling his slot, but the show's simply not the same. Few would take issue with the widely-held notion that no one can cajole, tease, and serve as straight man to Johnny Carson as well as McMahon can. More than just the show's announcer, McMahon is an outstanding second banana who could easily be first on his own.

In an interview on UPI Radio, McMahon summed up Carson's attitude toward his staff members' outside activities: "He is like the father of a little family of chickens, and some of the chickens are doing well. If Doc goes out and appears with the London Philharmonic, he loves that. If I go out and do something, he loves that . . . he's very proud of that."

On Sunday, February 5, 1978, the second banana would be first. He would reign supreme as Bacchus X.

Although (according to McMahon himself) his image as a boozer is grossly exaggerated, the people of New Orleans would rather think that it isn't. And so, his was a popular selection from the day it was announced. Who could be better to serve as the god of wine than one who has a reputation for imbibing quite a bit of the grape from time to time?

McMahon does not mind being kidded about his tendency toward spirits, but he calls it a myth that has been perpetuated too long. In fact, he has refused to play movie roles which glorify alcoholic consumption. Ralph Romaguera says that during "Mr. Budweiser's" reign, he carried a beer can almost everywhere, but it was "filled only with water."

Although the citizens of "the city that care forgot" were generous in their praise for the selection, a few krewe members wondered if Carson's straight man could produce in the role of top attraction. Member Charles Slater, a personal friend of the 1978 king, had no doubts. It was a silly concern: the king had had his share of lead roles in movies, had emceed television shows with panache and had successfully filled in as "Tonight Show" host in dire emergencies.

Guess who whips up the audience in a warm-up session before Carson appears to reap the benefits of a loose, responding group? Ed McMahon. And sell? Ed can sell Alpo like it was beef bourguignon. Someone once said he sells himself by being himself. His subjects would be solidly sold on Bacchus Sunday.

One could tell by his letter of acceptance that he considered his selection an honor:

November 14, 1977

Mr. Pete Moss
Executive Vice President
BACCHUS
P.O. Box 6309
New Orleans, Louisiana
70114

Dear Pete:

I am absolutely thrilled at your invitation to reign as the 1978 King of Bacchus. . . .
All good wishes and my sincerest thanks to you and the Krewe of Bacchus for this great honor.

Cordially,

ED McMAHON

Dr. Hugh Oser called the new king "our best publicity ever." The krewe board was convinced that McMahon's reign would enhance Bacchus's national image. And its members were right; during the days preceding and following his trip to New Orleans, millions heard Carson kid his sidekick about his ascendancy to royalty.

When the national media reported on Carnival 1978, Ed McMahon was prominently mentioned as king of the Krewe of Bacchus. With his high recognition factor, news reports and features attracted wide attention, and Bacchus benefited.

The Superdome Extravaganza, added to the Bacchus venue three years before, had almost become a tradition. However, Dome participants complained about the long wait as the parade traveled from the Rivergate to their indoor party. Guests at the Rivergate Rendezvous likewise had to wait even longer for the parade to return to its starting point.

In an effort to please, the krewe decided to start the procession at the Dome, thereby hoping to satisfy both complaints. The crowd of thirty thousand began to pour into the massive facility as soon as the gates were opened at 3:30 on

BACCHUS X

Sunday afternoon. Not only did Extravaganza ticketholders get to see the start of the parade, but they were also able to watch the krewe members board the floats. Doubloons were showered upon the fans before the floats that encircled the arena moved an inch.

When Ed McMahon mounted the king's float, a chant of "Bacchus, Bacchus, Bacchus" erupted. More than one Irish Channel accent could be heard in the crowd ("Hey, dawlin', ain't he gawgeous?"). As the tractors that pulled the floats revved their engines to depart, the crowd became frenzied. The lights were lowered, and the spectacle, resembling an unfurling, unending ribbon, began to move out of the stadium. Bacchus X toasted his minions and threw kisses and doubloons to admirers.

Ed McMahon—no "second banana" tonight

Richard Simmons

As the floats departed, marching bands entered the arena, filling every inch of the Dome with heart-pounding sound. The party was only now beginning in earnest, with six hours of entertainment to follow. The show, billed as the greatest in the history of Mardi Gras, included appearances by local groups Wild Tchoupitoulas and the Neville Brothers, along with Wolfman Jack, the Shirelles, Elvin Bishop, Levon Helm, Dr. John, Paul Butterfield, Booker T and the MGs, and others.

MARDI GRAS AND BACCHUS

The sounds of the marching bands reverberated in the background as the twenty-two floats headed down a parade route that would take them along Girod, Loyola, and Howard to Lee Circle, then down St. Charles to Canal, where the parade turned away from the river and slithered through waves of people to a turnaround at Dorgenois Street. The parade then went back down Canal through the throngs and ended at the Rivergate.

To remind the city of Bacchus's staying power, members chose the theme "Monarchs and Memories." The nine kings from the krewe's formative years were featured in huge likenesses. Behind the king's float with the huge figure of Bacchus raising his cup to the crowd came the officers. Then, in order of their appearance, came: the title float; the likeness of Bacchus I, Danny Kaye; the theme float for the 1969 inaugural parade, "The Best Things in Life"; Bacchus II, Raymond Burr; "Remember When," the 1970 theme; Bacchus III, Jim Nabors; "Bacchus Salutes Mardi Gras," the 1971 theme; Bacchus IV, Phil Harris; 1972's "Bacchus's Book of Horrors"; the beloved "Bacchusaurus"; Bacchus V, Bob Hope; 1973's "Bacchus Goes to the Movies"; Bacchus VI, Glen Campbell; "Bacchus Reads the Comics," 1974; Bacchus VII, Jackie Gleason; "Bacchus's Circus Parade," the 1975 theme; Bacchus VIII, Perry Como; "Spirit of '76"; Bacchus IX, Henry Winkler; and "Happily Ever After," the theme of 1977's procession.

Of course, the Budweiser Clydesdales were there in honor of the brewery's favorite point man, and it wasn't coincidental that the god of wine was toasting his subjects with gulps from cans of beer that evening. (But whether the cans held beer or water, only Bacchus X himself knows.)

Ready for action

BACCHUS X

Officers' wives with escorts

Ed McMahon has been around, but like all kings, he was visibly awed, more than the people were. The crowds, twenty and thirty deep, clamored for a throw from the late-night personality. He was definitely the star of this "Tonight Show."

McMahon's wife, Victoria, says her husband has an uncanny memory for names, dates, and places. (He remembers that Judy Holliday was playing in "Bells Are Ringing" at the Shubert Theater on the day he was interviewed by Johnny Carson. How? It was on the marquee across the street from Johnny's office.) However, the king's memory would not have to be amazing to remember the name, Bacchus; the place, New Orleans; the date, February 5, 1978. And the "jewel on the Mississippi" would long remember Ed McMahon.

From Burbank, California, he would write the following heartfelt letter to the people of New Orleans via the *Times-Picayune:*

Editor:

Mardi Gras is over for another year, and I want to say thank you to the Krewe of Bacchus and all the citizens of New Orleans for the very great honor you bestowed upon me. I'd never been to New Orleans for Mardi Gras before, and it certainly proved a fantastic initiation to participate my first time as King of Bacchus.

As you all know, I truly love your city, and have long felt that it's my home away from home.

I was particularly impressed and moved by the warmth, the enthusiasm, and the feelings of genuine love emanating from all of you fine people.

You've given me a time that I will long remember and cherish, and again, I thank you.

ED McMAHON

CHAPTER SIXTEEN

Bacchus XI, 1979
Happy Days—Almost

As the floats circle the supper dance assembly at the Rivergate, the crowd appears to be even more frenzied than in past years. Actor-director-writer Ron Howard, "Richie Cunningham" of the television show "Happy Days," looks stately and royal in his robes. The crowd reacts with gusto as Bacchus IX, Henry Winkler, assists the new king in toasting his subjects. On board the king's float are "Happy Days" regulars Donny Most (Ralph Malph), Tom Bosley (Howard Cunningham), and Marion Ross (Marion Cunningham), and Garry Marshall, creator and producer of the superhit sitcom. Ross is proud to be the first woman to ride in a Bacchus parade. A deluge of doubloons rains on the revelers below. The parade marshal gives the signal, and the parade comes to a halt. The procession has been a hit.

The difference: the parade marshal's and king's floats make up the entire parade. The route: once around the inside of the Rivergate. Why?

Carnival 1979 was not one of New Orleans' finest hours.

For several years, city police had threatened to strike just before Mardi Gras, knowing full well that havoc would result from the lack of law enforcement. The threat had always been a major bargaining chip. Until 1979, reason had apparently prevailed. However, when the Police Association of Louisiana became affiliated with the Teamsters Union, a much more militant attitude became prevalent. Each time the city council met a union demand, another was made.

Frustrated, Councilman-at-large Sidney Barthelemy told reporters, "At each level of negotiation, the demands have been increased. The first demand was recognition of PANO (Patrolman's Association of New Orleans). We recognized PANO. The second demand was restoring the sick and annual leave benefits. Done. The third demand was to get a different rank other than sergeant within the Patrolman's Association . . . another . . . was double time-and-a-half for overtime on holidays. Agreed. Restore tenure. Agreed.

The wives of Winkler and Howard see parade through top of limo

"What else must we, as city officials, agree to, other than say, 'here, you run city government, you don't need us, who are elected representatives of the people.' "

In a show of unity, the other councilmen raised their voices in defense of their position. "Where does the ante stop?" Mike Early asked. "They don't need a blank check signed by us now," Philip Ciaccio chimed in. Frank Friedler, Jr., felt the unreasonable demands were coming from an out-of-town negotiator, apparently referring to Teamsters International representative Joseph Valenti, who was brought in to conduct negotiations on behalf of the local affiliate.

The council refused to retreat any farther, the union went on strike, and Carnival and Mardi Gras 1979 were in great jeopardy. Every day, parades scheduled in New Orleans had to be canceled. Other organizations lived with the jitters of uncertainty, too. Still, the mayor and council refused to budge. In spite of a court injunction ordering strikers back to work, the walkout continued.

Union members clearly believed it was a bluff when rumors surfaced saying that all parades in Orleans Parish would be canceled. The rumors turned out to be true. On February 20—just one week before Mardi Gras—the captains of all of the major New Orleans krewes, declaring that they refused to let Carnival be

Howard gets a few pointers

Winkler and friends

held hostage in the five-day-old strike, called off all parades in the Crescent City for the remainder of the Carnival season.

Kaput. Finis. Parades and police were out, the Louisiana National Guard was in, and a newspaper editorial called New Orleans "a city under siege." Union bosses and members reacted in anger; their lever had been taken away.

Attempts were made to pick up the pieces. Some organizations took their processions to the suburbs. Indoor bashes were held throughout the city, including "Mardi Gras at the Superdome," billed as "the world's biggest disco." Ron Howard, Henry Winkler and other members of the "Happy Days" contingent made a brief appearance at the party. On the way to the Rivergate, Winkler, who had provided an Oscar-quality performance as Bacchus IX two years before, lamented friend Ron Howard's abridged reign. Refusing to comment on the labor-management impasse, Winkler noted that there was a definite lack of spirit in the city, but that the Bacchus people were just as excited as they were during his reign in 1977. It was still party time!

Ron Howard, whose father-in-law is from Gueydan, Louisiana, had never been to the Crescent City before. He would surely remember his first visit. New Orleanians will find any excuse for a good party, and the troubled city outside the Rivergate was no obstruction to the merrymaking inside the facility. The bacchanals refused to let the world of reality interfere completely with the make-believe world of Carnival. They drank, they danced, they feasted. Attired in formal dress, they fought for doubloons and beads like red-blooded New Orleanians are expected to do.

When the sirens and bright lights went on, attention turned to the abbreviated parade. From his glittering float, Bacchus XI boasted, "It looks like you can cancel the parades, but you can't cancel Mardi Gras." His following agreed. As if to make up for the traditional Carnival and Mardi Gras that had been denied them, they celebrated as if the season of joy might never return.

It had taken World War II to cancel the parades last time. Crime waves, Union troops, national scandals, carpetbaggers and World War I had been responsible for pre-empting the world-renowned festival at other times. Labor strife would now have to be added to that list.

During the strike threats, the mayor, council, business leaders, and krewe captains had all speculated on the dire ramifications of a canceled Carnival. In attempts to soften the union's position, the officials' darkly-painted scenarios grew more ominous with each statement. Following the police controversy, Mayor Morial and the city council worked hard to restore harmony with the police. With that accomplished, revelers could again feel secure on the streets during Carnival and Mardi Gras. The year 1980 proved all the doomsaying exaggerated, as the largest outdoor party in the world—Carnival—bounced back with the sort of elasticity that has made New Orleans one of America's (and the world's) unique cities.

And the actor with staying power who began playing "Opie" at age four on "The Andy Griffith Show" would be remembered as a well-loved king who had made the best of his retrenched reign.

Garry Marshall and the Winklers having fun

Howard with newsmen and admirers at airport

"Happy Days" cast arrives at Brennan's

Crowd in Superdome welcomes Howard

CHAPTER SEVENTEEN

Bacchus XII, 1980
Swing Low,
Sweet Clarinet

On October 13, 1979, over four months before the reign of Bacchus XII, an announcement identifying the 1980 Bacchus kings was made by the krewe.

Kings? That's right; the unpredictable krewe, widely recognized for breaking Carnival tradition, was now bending its own customs in more ways than one. There would be two kings, and they would not be from Hollywood.

While the appointed ones, Al Hirt and Pete Fountain, had achieved national fame, selecting the city's most celebrated contemporary musicians marked the first time that the krewe looked away from movie and television ranks for a king. Make that kings. Co-kings?

The news was well-received by press and public alike. A Bacchus spokesman said, "We feel that if anybody has done a lot for this city, it's Al and Pete, and we wanted to do something to honor them." The smiling rulers-to-be were photographed, bearded chin to bearded chin.

Hirt responded to reporters with pride. "It's a great thing to honor two local boys like this, and I know Brother Fountain feels the same way. It's a great honor. This will be the first time I've ridden in a parade since my unfortunate accident. And that's what it was, an accident." (Hirt says he was hit in the face by a piece of brick while riding in the 1970 Bacchus parade. One story circulating at the time had the trumpeter slipping or falling and hitting his mouth on the float stanchion. Hirt has continued to protest the rumor. Whatever the cause, the incident received a lot of bad press all across America the next morning.) Hirt jokingly asked the Bacchus people to put him high up on the king's float in 1980, because he didn't want to give anyone else another shot.

Peter Dewey LaFontaine, Jr., was equally touched, telling the *Times-Picayune,* "I'm speechless." Well, not quite. Fountain recovered enough to say, "When they called me about it, I thought they wanted me to be a page or something. But to be Bacchus, or whatever, that's got to be one of the highlights of my career and my life. Really.

MARDI GRAS AND BACCHUS

"I'm very big with Carnival anyway. We've been doing the Half-Fast Marching Club for twenty-one years now. But to live here in New Orleans and get to reign as Bacchus . . . I don't have the right words to tell you how I feel."

Krewe member M. "Squatty" Lowell remembers Fountain looking ahead to the Bacchus bash and doing a little wishful thinking. "If only I could have Lawrence Welk's liver for one night," Fountain moaned.

The acceptance speeches from New Orleans' two most prominent musical ambassadors sounded great. But there is, indeed, many a slip between the cup and the lip. When Bacchus rolled on February 17, 1980, there was only one king after all: Pete Fountain. In the interim, Al Hirt had decided not to participate. Why? Krewe leaders prefer not to elaborate, saying only that the trumpeter was insisting on special considerations. For whatever reason, he declined to occupy the throne with his longtime friend Pete Fountain.

Fountain was a true star as Bacchus XII, just as he was as a musician. The man whose boyhood respiratory problems led him to a life of music (his family doctor had prescribed clarinet-playing to strengthen his lungs) demonstrated that he could handle the reins of "power" with ease.

Reigning as Bacchus was a long way from hanging out at the old Top Hat Dance Club near his childhood home on Broad Street. From the Junior Dixie Band to the Opera House Burlesque Theater (replacing legendary jazzman Irving Fazola) to Phil Zito's International Dixieland Express, Fountain's career had been one of starts and sputters. It certainly wasn't because of a lack of talent; instead, it was because music tastes vacillated like rudderless clippers. The public's appreciation of jazz came and went.

It was a two-year contract with Lawrence Welk that propelled Fountain to national acclaim, as fast as "uh-one and uh-two and uh-three": overnight, the New Orleanian had "uh" national band and "uh" national audience that appreciated "uh" talent without equal.

But the smells, sounds, sights, and people of New Orleans kept calling. Soon he was back in his own club, Pete Fountain's French Quarter Inn. In 1977, he moved to a re-created replica of that club in the New Orleans Hilton. His reception and success there have been tremendous.

On Bacchus Sunday 1980, Peter the Great was given the reception of his life. It was one thing when Perry Como demonstrated a closeness with his group of fans, or when Henry Winkler turned his younger followers on. But Bacchus XII was a hometown boy. Many in the streets had seen him grow up. They shared and reveled in his success and admired him for handling his prominence with humility. It was not love at first sight for the bacchanals in the streets; it was a love that had begun long before and had grown through the years.

All along the parade route, from Napoleon Avenue along St. Charles to Canal and finally to the Rivergate, the love shone through. Ralph Romaguera remembered, "The New Orleans boy was a great king. He did everything and anything that was asked."

Responding to pleas for a simplified parade route—the long, spread-out route had almost paralyzed traffic in the city during recent parades—the krewe

The Fountain family

skipped the Superdome party and avoided the complicated maze of years past. The more-direct procession to the Rivergate did not diminish the number of spectators, thanks to a clever parade theme, "The Undersea World of Bac-Chu-Steau," which had been planned for the previous year's canceled procession.

On the lead float, King Fountain sat on his royal throne, the huge figure of the mythological god of wine joining him. Next came the officers' float and the theme float, followed by: "Neptune," "Deep Sea Divers," "Delicious Crustaceans," "Oysters and Pearls," "Louisiana Fishing," "Davey Jones' Locker," "Birds of the Sea," "Maine Lobsters," "Bacchusaurus," "Beautiful Mermaids," "Arctic Seas," "Deep-Sea Fishing," "Loch Ness Monster," "Sharks and Coral Reefs," "Sailing Ships," "Lost Atlantis," "Whales and Dolphins," and "Buccaneers of the Sea."

The previous year's canceled parade was all but forgotten as Fountain played some of his favorites at the Rivergate Rendezvous—favorites like "Licorice Stick" and "South Rampart Street Parade." He was generous with both talent and time.

The 1980 parade proved to be fatal to the huge, head-wagging Bacchusaurus I. On the way back to its den across the Mississippi River after the procession, the tipsy creature was set afire by a passing vandal as the $35,000 float stopped before crossing the bridge. The lovable likeness of a dinosaur, part of Bacchus since the krewe's inception twelve years before, had won the hearts of children of every age. Riding in barrels attached to its sides, krewe members had thrown barrels of doubloons to merrymakers.

Krewe member Harold Hughes remembered the time someone forgot to close the toilet drain on the float and "Bacchusaurus 'urinated' [during] the

Fountain with Gary Burghoff

Fountain prepares for the parade

whole parade." Hughes called it an "eye-watering experience." A new Bacchusaurus would appear the next year to make more memories.

The next morning, the *Times-Picayune* reported on the successful reign of Bacchus XII. Also on the newspaper's pages were frustrating stories about the plight of American hostages in Iran. The drama being acted out halfway around the world would play a part in the selection of Bacchus XIII.

Fountain plays for pages

BACCHUS RENDEZVOUS

THE OLD TESTAMENT

NEW ORLEANS
MARDI GRAS MARCH 1, 1981

Frolich

© 1980 AGMPANY FROLICH AND BLAINE KERN ARTISTS INC

CHAPTER EIGHTEEN

Bacchus XIII, 1981 From the Halls of Montezuma . . .

Who would have thought that the Ayatollah Khomeini, Iranian President Abolhassan Bani-Sadr (later exiled), and a group of assorted terrorists would have a hand in picking Bacchus XIII?

The teetotaling, self-declared chief Imam would probably order the dawn execution of ninety percent of New Orleans's population for merely attending a pagan feast like Carnival. Yet he and his government were responsible for creating fifty-three American heroes, one of whom—Sergeant John D. McKeel, Jr.—would reign as the mythological god of wine in 1981.

Riding as escorts to the king would be eight other marine hostages: Staff Sergeant Michael Moerrer and Sergeants James M. Lopez, William Gallegos, Rodney Sickmann, Kevin Hermening, Steven Kirtley, Paul E. Lewis, and Gregory A. Persinger. Fourteen other former hostages would be guests of radio station WWL.

There were some who saw the selection of a second successive non-Hollywood Bacchus as a sign of weakness in the krewe's ability to attract big names. To others, it meant only that Bacchus was mature enough, confident enough to take chances, to vote with the heart instead of the head.

Without apology, a Bacchus spokesman explained: "In the old scheme of things, the Sunday night before Mardi Gras was a dead night. We felt we needed a parade to keep interest and enthusiasm soaring as a fitting prelude to the big day. We also thought Mardi Gras needed national and international publicity. And one way to get that was to have a prominent figure as king of the parade and festivities.

"Each year, a committee meets to select a potential king. Primarily, we seek to invite someone who deserves the honor . . . either through service, charity or personal sacrifice. In 1981, we thought New Orleans should pay homage to the ex-hostages who had sacrificed 444 days of their lives in confinement under dangerous, demeaning and depriving circumstance.

"Attracting the celebrity the committee wants is, of course, not a *fait accompli*. You don't simply say, 'Let's get Margaret Thatcher or Prince Philip.' "

He used the occasion to clarify a common misconception: that Bacchus pays a fee to its kings. "Simply stated," he said, "they come because it is an honor. Expenses only are paid and, naturally, the king and his entourage are entertained royally. Family members and friends are invited at the expense of the krewe, but the king gets *no fee!*" He punctuated the latter statement in mock frustration.

The krewe leader pointed out that celebrities of the caliber invited by Bacchus do not expect a fee. "If we had approached Bob Hope with money, the honor would have been gone. And now, when we approach someone and they learn that Bob came for honor's sake only, they recognize the prestige of following in his footsteps."

The Bacchus spokesman said one of the major problems is explaining Bacchus to the prospective king. "Actually, they never fully understand until they participate.

"When Bob Hope was asked to describe to Sergeant McKeel his feelings about having been king of Bacchus, he did so with magnanimity, explaining how the marine was being inducted into a very small and exclusive group. You can bet McKeel listened."

A riding lieutenant with the San Diego Chicken, 1981

Officers getting ready

McKeel with Pete Fountain

Inducted he was! Dressed in his military uniform as he requested, the stone-faced twenty-seven-year-old marine was spit and polish to the core. The sergeant had made the national news on his release when someone asked him what he was looking forward to doing. Without flinching, the bachelor replied that he was anxious to get back to chasing women. When his hometown organized a parade for him soon thereafter, the Dallas Cowboys Cheerleaders were there. But he regretted that they were too far behind in the procession for him to appreciate, let alone chase.

McKeel's parents and over a half million proud Americans were on hand to see the nine marines. All along the parade route, from Napoleon via St. Charles to Canal and the Rivergate, the king and his court threw doubloons to the spectators, who responded by gently pitching back chilled cans of beer.

The theme of the parade that year was "Welcome Home," with the title, "The Old Testament, 1981."

Following the king's, theme, title, and officers' floats came: "The Creation," "The Garden of Eden," "Nebuchadnezzar," "Noah's Ark," "Abraham, Father of Nations," "Sodom and Gomorrah—Lot's Wife," "Moses in the Bullrushes," "The Plagues of Egypt," "The Parting of the Red Sea," the new "Bacchusaurus," "The Ten Commandments," "Joshua and the Battle of Jericho," "Samson," "David and Goliath," "Jacob's Ladder," "The Wisdom of King Solomon," "Daniel in the Lion's Den," "Jonah and the Whale" and "Follow the Star."

The welcome-home celebration was marred when a wild gunman at Canal and Royal streets wounded two bandsmen in the parade—one from Tulane University and one from St. Augustine High School. The twenty-two floats kept ambling on to the Rivergate.

Lending a helping hand

Pat Barberot plays

McKeel meets page

There was ample toasting of the former hostages at the Rendezvous. In true Marine Corps spirit, they responded with gulps of beer rather than wine.

To these men, who had been held captive for over fourteen months, the stay in New Orleans was too good to be true. It had the flavor of make-believe: brunches at the Court of Two Sisters and the Hilton Hotel; dinners at Brennan's, the Rib Room, and Anything Goes; a Pete Fountain show and a Famous Door jazz party—to name just a few functions. For former Marine Rodney "Rocky" Sickmann (he apparently had been discharged by then), it was like a real fairy tale as he proposed to his sweetheart, Jill Ditch, during his visit. The couple announced their engagement to one hundred Bacchus members during the dinner at Brennan's.

The royal treatment of the marines was a far cry from the treatment they had received in Tehran. One wavering, thick-tongued bacchanal invented a toast to the Ayatollah: "For all you do, this burp's for you." The crowd roared back at the sound of relief.

© 1981 A COMPANY FROLICH AND BLAINE KERN ARTISTS, INC.

CHAPTER NINETEEN

Bacchus XIV, 1982 "Eat Your Heart Out, Burt"

After two years of non-Hollywood kings, the Krewe of Bacchus allayed all fears that it might be losing its touch with the announcement that actor-comedian Dom DeLuise would reign as Bacchus XIV.

On Bacchus Sunday, there was an instant rapport between ruler and ruled. V. L. Mayer, Jr., describes the king performing an "ice-breaking" gesture that left members rolling with laughter in their very first encounter. Mayer says DeLuise told the Reverend Peter Rogers in the dressing room that, although it had been the priest's place to bless the people on that Sunday morning, it was *his* turn now to bless his flock on Sunday evening. The grand comic dipped his portable microphone in Pete Fountain's cocktail and began sprinkling "spirited water" on the assembled members.

If the people of New Orleans liked the hilarious cherub as much as krewe members did, public opinions on the selection must have been almost unanimous. When asked to name and describe their favorite king, krewe members were generous in their praise of Bacchus XIV.

"Dom DeLuise looked like Bacchus incarnate," according to Dr. James T. Riley; "He was very enthusiastic and seemed to really enjoy himself and appreciate the honor," said Wayne Kempff; "He best personified a people's Mardi Gras king who embodied the wild, uninhibited fun that is a foundation of our parade," stated Jeff Martin, son of and rider for Ken Martin.

Herman Frank was impressed because DeLuise came to each float's dressing area in the Rivergate, a sentiment echoed by Harold D. Magee, Jr.: "He spent more time in the krewe's quarters than [any of the] other kings." V. L. Mayer, Jr. voted for DeLuise because "of his friendliness and enthusiasm before, during and after the parade. He provided more laughs for members, crowd and guests." Jack Duarte said, "He epitomized the correct way a King of Bacchus should act. EVERYONE loved him." And float lieutenant Donald Strain called Bacchus XIV a "great personality" and "down-to-earth."

Another float lieutenant, Conrad Spatz, saw DeLuise as "genuine and sincere in his response to the honor. Even non-members felt he had a flair for displaying the enjoyment of being king."

To Geoffrey Boulmay, Jr., the comedian "seemed more relaxed with all members, laughing and joking . . . and not confining himself [away] from the regular membership."

Wayne Barrett enumerated his reasons for picking DeLuise: "1) He stayed longer than any other king, 2) he entertained the krewe, and 3) [he] enjoyed himself." Jeffrey Doussan submitted a similar list, saying that the king was personable with members and the crowd at the parade, "complimented our city," and "acted the part well."

Float lieutenant Ted Sternberg was of the opinion that this celebrity was "just what a Bacchus king should be—fun-loving and outgoing . . . a real showman."

On and on went the positive comments, with the words almost sounding like echoes. John Carpenter called him a great "comic." Richard McCloskey: "Outgoing." Float lieutenant M. J. Robichaux, Jr.: "Personable . . . enthusiasm . . . thankful." Another float lieutenant, Eddie Boehm: "Funny . . . down-to-earth." E. J. Waguespack, Jr.: "Likeable." Earnest Clark: "Warm and available." Robert Abramson: "Amusing." Dr. A. J. Celino: "For real . . . courteous . . . friendly."

At the risk of sounding repetitious: "Very personable"—H. J. Romero III; "More down-to-earth"—R. J. Melancon, Jr.; "Super personality"—William J. Sansovich; "Friend of the krewe from the beginning"—Harold Hughes.

"Mixed with the crowd during the ball"—W. G. Pergande; "Happy to be king"—J. Levine; "Personality and friendliness"—Louis DiRosa, Jr.; "Personal involvement and generosity"—Edwin F. Stacy, Jr.; "Related to all the people"—

"We Three Kings": DeLuise, Jim Nabors, Fountain

DeLuise receives king's medallion from krewe captain

DeLuise during airport interview

Thomas W. Capo; "Appeal[ed] to all classes, races"—Greg Sterk; "More enthusiasm into the role than any other"—Ronald J. Hebert.

To the relish of hundreds of thousands, King Dom played the jester as much as the king. His was a charismatic relationship with the people in the crowd, whose comments were along the lines of "my gawd, hon, he's having so much fun you'd think he's from Nu Awlins." (To the outsider, there are more than a few similarities between DeLuise's native Brooklynese and the typical "Nu Awlins" accent.)

The theme of the parade was "American Heroes and Heroines." First came Bacchus XIV in all his might and splendor. The officers followed on the theme float. Then came the floats depicting heroes and heroines: "Jim Thorpe," "Mark Twain," "Andrew Jackson," "Midnight Riders," "Pecos Bill," "George Washington," "Johnny Appleseed," "Louis Armstrong," "Pocahontas," "Paul Bunyan," "Jean Lafitte," "Paul Revere," "Robert E. Lee," "Daniel Boone," "Betsy Ross," "General Patton," "Kit Carson," "Columbus" and "Casey Jones." The regulars—"Bacchusaurus," "King Kong" and "Queen Kong"—were joined by "Baby Kong."

Member Ronald J. Hebert related this parade anecdote: "One can usually receive kisses along the parade route in exchange for long "pearl" beads [thrown by members]. A fellow float rider was doing just that, and in the hustle-bustle of the crowd, the kiss was planted onto his eye instead of his kisser. The power of the kiss was such that it sucked one of his contact lens out of his eye. Lost forever. As it turned out, he might as well have given away a real pearl necklace."

Captain August Perez III said a million doubloons were thrown that night, and DeLuise drew a million laughs as he clowned from the Garden District to Canal and the Rivergate.

In front of Gallier Hall, DeLuise did an impromptu bump and grind, to the delight of the thousands packed around the float like worker bees around their queen. When the master of ceremonies, City Councilman Mike Early, announced to the crowd that DeLuise had been selected over his good friend Burt Reynolds because of his "beauty and wit," DeLuise yelled out, "Eat your heart out, Burt." And the parade rolled on.

New member Herman Frank recalled his most vivid memory of his first Bacchus ride: "Turning into Canal Street and seeing what seemed to be an infinite number with their hands in the air and their screams echoing in my ears."

It was also the first Bacchus parade ride for new member J. Al McElroy, Jr. He had been married for only twenty-four hours. He said, "That was interesting!" and gave credit to a "very understanding young bride."

Float sergeant Edward Wedge, Jr., noticed that as the last floats rolled by, many paradegoers were indifferent to catching or picking up throws; their appetites had been satisfied by the preceding floats.

King's aide Jesse Stanton helps in crowning ritual

Krewe members before parade

The king had gained acting experience with major roles in *Blazing Saddles, Cannonball Run, Silent Movie, Smokey and the Bandit II,* and *The Best Little Whorehouse in Texas.* But none had prepared him for the role he played as Bacchus and the hysteria he witnessed on his ride down Canal.

After the parade, not only did DeLuise perform on stage at the Rivergate Rendezvous, but he was also "available" to one and all after his entertainment spot.

Among the first fifteen Bacchus kings, the fourteenth would later be voted one of the krewe members' big favorites. Ralph Romaguera was high on DeLuise's reign: "It's hard to say who was the best king ever, but Dom has to be tied with whomever. He was funny, great, and loved the crowds. He went up to a strange lady and asked for an earring to finish off his outfit. When waiting in the limo, DeLuise overheard a young boy asking a friend if he thought Dom would give him an autograph. The king opened the door and granted the boy his wish.

"At the Saturday night officers party, Dom asked me to photograph him at each table. The guests loved it. During the party, the band announced, 'Mr. Dom DeLuise to head the second line!' Dom turned to me and asked, 'What the hell is a second line?' I said, 'Someone will give you an umbrella; dance around like a fool!' 'I can handle that,' he said, adding, 'These people are crazy!' "

Ralph's favorite Bacchus photograph is one of Dom dancing with his mother.

Bacchus's latest celebrity king had been a big smash. Could the krewe keep up the good work in its '83 selection? Stay tuned!

(Meanwhile, Al McElroy resumed his honeymoon.)

CHAPTER TWENTY

Bacchus XV, 1983
He Looked Like a King

In 1983, the big question was, could the Krewe of Bacchus attract another celebrity king of Dom DeLuise's caliber? The answer would be a resounding "yes."

When Charlton Heston mounted the king's float on February 13, he was Ben Hur, Moses, and John the Baptist rolled into one in the eyes of his subjects, who had seen him in all these roles. (In the movie *Buccaneer,* he had also played the close-to-home part of General Andrew Jackson at the Battle of New Orleans.)

On Bacchus Sunday '83, he was whatever the eyes of the beholder wanted him to be. And to the membership, he was something special.

There is a large portrait of the Hollywood king in full Bacchus regalia adorning the entrance to the studio of Bacchus photographer Ralph Romaguera. The photograph is so imposing, Napoleon Bonaparte would cringe from the power of it all. Krewe members who voted for Heston as their favorite king felt the force of his captivating regal manner:

"He looked and played the part of a king," said J. Eirich, Jr.

"He gave the Krewe a certain 'class' because of his stature," according to Michael Levy.

Speaking of class, float lieutenant Edward R. Wedge, Jr. declared: "His demeanor and bearing lent class to his role as Bacchus. A class organization had a class king."

Donald Bauman liked Heston best because "he was regal," while Rubin Chandler felt "he more fitted the role as king." O. K. LeBlanc approved of "his kingly manner," and float sergeant Michael Lanier saw a "gracious image."

While Heston received a large percentage of votes for projecting a royal stance, there were quite a few who applauded his personable, friendly, and gracious manner.

Float sergeant Griff Harrell liked the fact that "he was personable, interested," and "didn't insist on being treated like a prima donna."

"He was stately yet friendly. Personable yet godlike"—like Bacchus himself, said float lieutenant Greg Federico.

Heston was George Pitre's favorite king because of "his friendliness, his image . . . and his personal way."

Norman J. Glindmeyer summarized it succinctly: "My favorite king was Charlton Heston, because he *was* Bacchus!"

On that February Sunday, the star of the Oscar-winning movie *The Greatest Show on Earth* saw that Carnival really is the greatest show on Earth, a show in which several hundred thousand actors participate every year.

The parade route was fairly direct: from Napoleon to Canal via St. Charles and ending at the Rivergate Rendezvous. Conditions for the parade were perfect. The sky was clear, the temperature was mild, and emotions were typically intense.

James T. Riley, a new member and first-time rider, described a scene that would be etched on his mind forever. "When a Bacchus cup was thrown to the sea of hands on Canal Street, it would bounce, roll and travel exactly as if it were in ocean waves."

Michael Levy thought the 1983 parade was the best he had experienced. "We outdrew Rex on the street. I attended Endymion and Rex as a spectator, and the crowds weren't even close to what I saw from my float."

The *Times-Picayune* was likewise impressed. "Bacchus proved once again to be one of Carnival's biggest draws, thousands packed in like sardines along the

Heston receives parade instructions

Heston and new friends

Heston with Shari Lewis and Lamb Chop

Heston with police

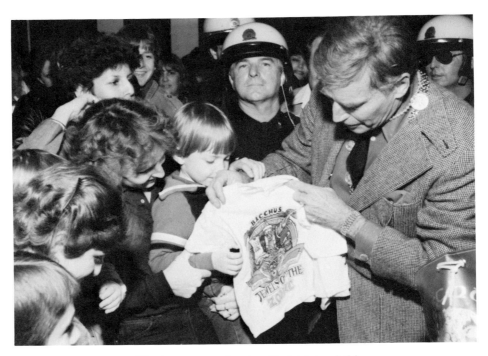

Heston pauses to give T-shirt to child

parade route rooting for a spot close enough to grab the throws generously thrown from riders on the twenty-six floats.

"Others stepped on toes and squeezed in closer to get a glimpse of movie star Charlton Heston."

Throughout the dazzling procession, the nobleman toasted his kingdom from atop his chariot-throne, as if being a leader was second nature. Ralph Romaguera maintained, "Nobody has been more 'kingly.' " The photographer was impressed when the king "willingly gave his time to the people [including] a visit to the Children's Hospital." He continued, "He was most agreeable . . . nothing less than a first-class act for Bacchus."

The lead float was trailed by twenty-five additional giant, animated displays that carried out the astrological theme. After Heston came the theme float, "Jewels of the Zodiac," followed by the officers' float, then "January," "Capricorn," "February," "Pisces," "March," "April," "Taurus," "May," "Gemini," "June," "Bacchusaurus," "King Kong," "Queen Kong," "Baby Kong," "Cancer," "July," "Leo," "August," "September," "October," "November," "Sagittarius," and "December."

The kingly yet personable aura followed the king into the Rendezvous, and the bacchanals were plainly in awe of their leader.

If Ben Hur had driven his chariot down Canal Street, if Moses had parted the Mississippi River, or if Andrew Jackson's statue in the square had suddenly come to life, Rendezvous participants would not have been impressed more. With Charlton Heston as its leader, Bacchus had pulled off another *coup de grace.*

CHAPTER TWENTY-ONE

Bacchus XVI, 1984
An International Affair

The Bacchus spectacle of 1984 had all the trimmings of international attention and flavor the krewe had hoped for in the beginning. In tribute to the 1984 World Exposition, scheduled to open in New Orleans nine weeks later, the parade motif mirrored the fair theme, "Rivers of the World." It was a production that would have astounded the most optimistic of krewe founders in 1968 when they had set out to do the impossible.

Nineteen nations and their famed rivers were featured on floats in the lavish display: "The Nile, Egypt"; "Seine, France"; "Yukon, Canada"; "Amazon, Brazil"; "Orinoco, Venezuela"; "Mississippi, United States"; "Aragon, Spain"; "Jordan, Israel"; "Yangtze, China"; "Danube, Austria"; "Rio Grande, Mexico"; "Rhine, Germany"; "Congo, Africa"; "Po, Italy"; "Volga, Russia"; "Thames, England"; "Shannon, Ireland"; "Kwai, Indonesia"; and "Ganges, India."

Of course, the Kong family was there to dazzle children of all ages, but the eyes of New Orleans were riveted on the powerful personality occupying the throne on the king's float. Platitudes could hardly do justice to the pageant and crowd reaction, but they were fitting homage to the world citizen leading this global supershow.

Headlining the impressive array of twenty-two musical groups was the Louisiana State University Marching Band, accompanied by the Golden Girls from Tigerland.

The mass of humanity was also treated to costume pins, beads, cups, mugs, coasters, and megaphones. It was a far cry from the standard plastic necklaces of old. But mostly, the smiling, swaying crowd of revelers shoved and stretched to get a look at a bigger-than-life figure: Kirk Douglas. For those who had waited since midmorning to reserve a favorable vantage point, the wait was worth it.

Kirk Douglas, Bacchus XVI, is an international figure, a multi-faceted man whose contributions extend far beyond movie and television screens. Since 1947, not a single year has gone by without the release of a movie starring this

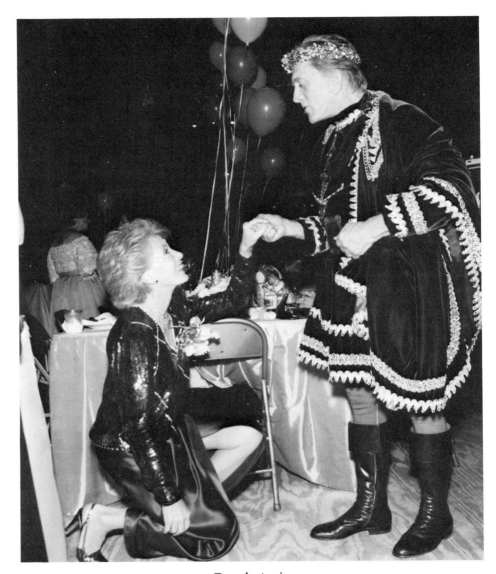

Douglas' reign

star of stars. And some have been box-office smashes: *Champion, The Bad and the Beautiful,* and *Lust for Life* all brought him Academy Award nominations.

There were other memorable performances in films like *Paths of Glory, Spartacus, Lonely Are the Brave,* and *Seven Days in May.* Douglas was the only American star in the Australian movie *The Man from Snowy River,* which broke all box-office records Down Under.

But movies are only one side of his many-faceted career. Another is public service, which to him is both opportunity and obligation. Since 1963, he has traveled the planet—from Japan to Mainland China, from Afghan refugee camps to Hong Kong—to seek to explain why America works and what freedom means.

Douglas and subject

Awards? There have been many: the Presidential Medal of Freedom, the highest award that can be conferred upon a private citizen; the Jefferson Award, for outstanding contributions to his country; the Cecil B. deMille Award, presented to him by the Hollywood Foreign Press Association for his world-wide contributions to the motion picture industry; and the prestigious Splendid American Award from the Thomas A. Dooley Foundation, for his humanitarian efforts. All of these and more have been bestowed upon this son of Russian immigrants.

Producer, director, actor nonpareil, ambassador of goodwill for his country . . . this is Kirk Douglas. This was Bacchus XVI—another master stroke for the Krewe of Bacchus and New Orleans. Although the reign of Douglas the Great took place after the 1983 membership survey, votes for Bacchus XVI would have stuffed the ballot box.

Who would next wear the Bacchus crown? Would it be Gregory Peck, Tom Selleck, Bob Newhart, Kenny Rogers, Sylvester Stallone, Alan Alda, Burt Reynolds, Peter Ustinov, Tom Jones, Paul Newman, Johnny Carson, Carol Burnett, Rodney Dangerfield, Clint Eastwood, Edwin Edwards, Jerry Lewis, Frank Sinatra, Mickey Rooney, George Burns, Sammy Davis, Jr., Chevy Chase, Fats Domino, Neil Diamond, Rich Little, Dudley Moore, Richard Pryor, Robin Williams, Dean Martin, Don Rickles, George Peppard, or Billy Joel? All of the above were submitted by members as suggestions to members of the board.

Some members suggested sports personalities. One wanted Tulane University's football coach for the team's recent victories over arch-rival Louisiana State University. Others nominated past and present New Orleans Saints quarterbacks Archie Manning and Ken Stabler.

Whoever the next and subsequent Bacchuses might be, they would have to go some to upstage the last three: DeLuise, Heston and Douglas. The krewe was definitely on a roll. Bacchus had arrived and was planning to stay.

Mardi Gras Dates

Year	Date	Year	Date	Year	Date	Year	Date	Year	Date
1801	Feb. 17	1856	Feb. 5	1911	Feb. 28	1966	Feb. 22	2021	Feb. 16
1802	Mar. 2	1857	Feb. 24	1912	Feb. 20	1967	Feb. 7	2022	Mar. 1
1803	Feb. 22	1858	Feb. 16	1913	Feb. 4	1968	Feb. 27	2023	Feb. 21
1804	Feb. 14	1859	Mar. 8	1914	Feb. 24	1969	Feb. 18	2024	Feb. 13
1805	Feb. 26	1860	Feb. 21	1915	Feb. 16	1970	Feb. 10	2025	Mar. 4
1806	Feb. 18	1861	Feb. 12	1916	Mar. 7	1971	Feb. 23	2026	Feb. 17
1807	Feb. 10	1862	Mar. 4	1917	Feb. 20	1972	Feb. 15	2027	Feb. 9
1808	Mar. 1	1863	Feb. 17	1918	Feb. 12	1973	Mar. 6	2028	Feb. 29
1809	Feb. 14	1864	Feb. 9	1919	Mar. 4	1974	Feb. 26	2029	Feb. 13
1810	Mar. 6	1865	Feb. 28	1920	Feb. 17	1975	Feb. 11	2030	Mar. 5
1811	Feb. 26	1866	Feb. 18	1921	Feb. 8	1976	Mar. 2	2031	Feb. 25
1812	Feb. 11	1867	Mar. 5	1922	Feb. 28	1977	Feb. 22	2032	Feb. 10
1813	Mar. 2	1868	Feb. 25	1923	Feb. 13	1978	Feb. 7	2033	Mar. 1
1814	Feb. 22	1869	Feb. 9	1924	Mar. 4	1979	Feb. 27	2034	Feb. 21
1815	Feb. 7	1870	Mar. 1	1925	Feb. 24	1980	Feb. 19	2035	Feb. 6
1816	Feb. 27	1871	Feb. 21	1926	Feb. 16	1981	Mar. 3	2036	Feb. 26
1817	Feb. 18	1872	Feb. 13	1927	Mar. 1	1982	Feb. 23	2037	Feb. 17
1818	Feb. 3	1873	Feb. 25	1928	Feb. 21	1983	Feb. 15	2038	Mar. 9
1819	Feb. 23	1874	Feb. 17	1929	Feb. 12	1984	Mar. 6	2039	Feb. 22
1820	Feb. 15	1875	Feb. 9	1930	Mar. 4	1985	Feb. 19	2040	Feb. 14
1821	Mar. 6	1876	Feb. 29	1931	Feb. 17	1986	Feb. 11	2041	Mar. 5
1822	Feb. 19	1877	Feb. 13	1932	Feb. 9	1987	Mar. 3	2042	Feb. 18
1823	Feb. 11	1878	Mar. 5	1933	Feb. 28	1988	Feb. 16	2043	Feb. 10
1824	Mar. 2	1879	Feb. 25	1934	Feb. 13	1989	Feb. 7	2044	Mar. 1
1825	Feb. 15	1880	Feb. 10	1935	Mar. 5	1990	Feb. 27	2045	Feb. 21
1826	Feb. 7	1881	Mar. 1	1936	Feb. 25	1991	Feb. 12	2046	Feb. 6
1827	Feb. 27	1882	Feb. 21	1937	Feb. 9	1992	Mar. 3	2047	Feb. 26
1828	Feb. 19	1883	Feb. 6	1938	Mar. 1	1993	Feb. 23	2048	Feb. 18
1829	Mar. 3	1884	Feb. 26	1939	Feb. 21	1994	Feb. 15	2049	Mar. 2
1830	Feb. 23	1885	Feb. 17	1940	Feb. 6	1995	Feb. 28	2050	Feb. 22
1831	Feb. 15	1886	Mar. 9	1941	Feb. 25	1996	Feb. 20	2051	Feb. 14
1832	Mar. 6	1887	Feb. 22	1942	Feb. 17	1997	Feb. 11	2052	Mar. 5
1833	Feb. 19	1888	Feb. 14	1943	Mar. 9	1998	Feb. 24	2053	Feb. 18
1834	Feb. 11	1889	Mar. 5	1944	Feb. 22	1999	Feb. 16	2054	Feb. 10
1835	Mar. 3	1890	Feb. 18	1945	Feb. 13	2000	Mar. 7	2055	Mar. 2
1836	Feb. 16	1891	Feb. 10	1946	Mar. 5	2001	Feb. 27	2056	Feb. 15
1837	Feb. 7	1892	Mar. 1	1947	Feb. 18	2002	Feb. 12	2057	Mar. 6
1838	Feb. 27	1893	Feb. 14	1948	Feb. 10	2003	Mar. 4	2058	Feb. 26
1839	Feb. 12	1894	Feb. 6	1949	Mar. 1	2004	Feb. 24	2059	Feb. 11
1840	Mar. 3	1895	Feb. 26	1950	Feb. 21	2005	Feb. 8	2060	Mar. 2
1841	Feb. 23	1896	Feb. 18	1951	Feb. 6	2006	Feb. 28	2061	Feb. 22
1842	Feb. 8	1897	Mar. 2	1952	Feb. 26	2007	Feb. 20	2062	Feb. 7
1843	Feb. 28	1898	Feb. 22	1953	Feb. 17	2008	Feb. 5	2063	Feb. 27
1844	Feb. 20	1899	Feb. 14	1954	Mar. 2	2009	Feb. 24	2064	Feb. 19
1845	Feb. 4	1900	Feb. 27	1955	Feb. 22	2010	Feb. 16	2065	Feb. 10
1846	Feb. 24	1901	Feb. 19	1956	Feb. 14	2011	Mar. 8	2066	Feb. 23
1847	Feb. 16	1902	Feb. 11	1957	Mar. 5	2012	Feb. 21	2067	Feb. 15
1848	Mar. 1	1903	Feb. 24	1958	Feb. 18	2013	Feb. 12	2068	Mar. 6
1849	Feb. 20	1904	Feb. 16	1959	Feb. 10	2014	Mar. 4	2069	Feb. 27
1850	Feb. 12	1905	Mar. 7	1960	Mar. 1	2015	Feb. 17	2070	Feb. 11
1851	Mar. 4	1906	Feb. 27	1961	Feb. 14	2016	Feb. 9	2071	Mar. 3
1852	Feb. 24	1907	Feb. 12	1962	Mar. 6	2017	Feb. 26	2072	Feb. 23
1853	Feb. 8	1908	Mar. 3	1963	Feb. 26	2018	Feb. 13	2073	Feb. 7
1854	Feb. 28	1909	Feb. 23	1964	Feb. 11	2019	Mar. 5	2074	Feb. 27
1855	Feb. 20	1910	Feb. 8	1965	Mar. 2	2020	Feb. 25	2075	Feb. 19